A Pictorial Guide to Southern Wagons and Vans

Terry Gough ARPS

© Kestrel Railway Books and Terry Gough 2007

Kestrel Railway Books
PO Box 269
SOUTHAMPTON
SO30 4XR

www.kestrelrailwaybooks.co.uk

No part of this publication may be reproduced, stored in a retrieval system, transmitted in any form or by any means, electronic, mechanical, or photocopied, recorded or otherwise, without the consent of the publisher in writing.

Printed by The Amadeus Press.

ISBN 978-1-905505-04-3

Front cover, top: Train of Southern wagons, left to right SR brake van No DS455 (diagram 1581), SR open wagon No 11093 (diagram 1400), SR designed cattle wagon No B891364 (diagram 1530) and SECR brake van No 55513 (diagram 1560) at Burnham on Crouch on 25th November 2005. (Terry Gough)

Front cover, bottom: SR milk tank No 4409 (diagram 3159) at Didcot on 21st January 2006. (Terry Gough)

Back cover, top: LBSCR open wagon No S27884 (diagram 1369) at Yeovil Junction on 22nd December 2005. (Terry Gough)

Back cover, bottom: LSWR brake van No 54885 (diagram 1541) at Washford on 6th June 2006. (Terry Gough)

CONTENTS

Introduction iii
Acknowledgments vii
Bibliography vii
List of Current Locations of Rolling Stock viii
Prefixes and Suffixes to Vehicle Numbers viii
Abbreviations viii
Chapter 1: Goods Vehicles 1
    Open Goods and Mineral Wagons 1
    Covered Goods Wagons 11
    Cattle Wagons and Special Cattle Vans 28
    Gunpowder Vans 37
    Goods Brake Vans 39
    Bolster Wagons 62
    Trucks (Vehicle, Machinery and Container) 67
Chapter 2: Engineers' Vehicles 81
    Brake Vans 82
    Ballast Wagons 86
Chapter 3: Passenger Vans 95
    Guard's Vans 97
    Ventilated Vans 111
    Luggage Vans 116
    Covered Carriage Trucks 125
    Milk Tankers 133
    Post Office Vans 139
Index 151

INTRODUCTION

This book serves as a reminder of the rolling stock of a bygone era, when the vast majority of goods vehicles consisted of wooden bodies on 4-wheeled underframes. A small number of such vehicles have survived and can be seen on various heritage railways, but many of them can only be recreated as models. I have concentrated on both these aspects in covering wagons and vans of the Southern Railway and its constituent companies.

Two events in the 1960s prompted me to show an interest in railway wagons. The first was the realisation that it was not only the steam locomotive that was rapidly disappearing from British Railways, but so too was the traditional goods wagon. Secondly and relevant to modelling, I found that although I could purchase kits for several of the more common Southern Railway and pre-grouping companies' locomotives, if I wanted to run realistic trains, then I would need to scratch build most of my rolling stock. I therefore set out to measure and photograph as many wagons as I could find. I was fortunate that, at the time, I lived in Woking with its busy yard to which I had access. I was also aware of the wealth of ancient rolling stock on the Isle of Wight, which I visited on numerous occasions. My general interest in railways took me to most parts of the Southern Region, so I always took the opportunity to photograph rolling stock as well as trains and stations. To augment my archives, I have recently visited several locations where Southern vehicles can still be seen. The nearest is under five miles from my home and the furthest is over 5,000 miles.

Much of the information I have gathered, particularly the photographs, has remained untouched in my files for over 40 years, apart from an occasional article in the model railway press. In the meantime the model trade has been transformed, with more locomotives in both kit and ready to run forms. The availability of rolling stock has also greatly improved and no longer is it necessary to build almost everything from scratch. There are, of course, many modellers who prefer building from scratch, or at least improving the accuracy and detail on ready to run vehicles.

In recent years several detailed historical accounts of Southern wagons have been published. I leave it to the reader to decide whether it is a coincidence that almost all the authors of these books also lived (and indeed still live) in the Woking area. These are excellent reference works and cover as far as is known virtually every wagon ever built for the Southern Railway and its constituent pre-grouping companies. For modellers the amount of information is perhaps overwhelming, both in terms of choice of vehicle and information thereon.

Within this book, I have used the terms wagon, van and truck, as far as possible based on their dictionary definitions. I refer to a wagon as an open railway vehicle designed for carrying goods and merchandise. A van is a covered wagon, and a truck is a vehicle for carrying a detachable item such as a container or a road vehicle. Passenger vans are those vehicles designed to run under the same operating conditions as passenger trains, but do not themselves carry passengers. This includes luggage vans, milk trucks and tanks, and horseboxes. To complicate the issue, some goods vehicles were uprated to run in passenger trains. One type of passenger van, with end doors, was referred to as a "covered carriage truck". Both the SR and BR used code names for some of their rolling stock. In particular BR used the names of mammals for its engineers' vehicles and these were applied to former SR vehicles. Following the introduction of the Total Operations Processing System (TOPS) in 1973, vehicles were given a three letter code indicating the type of vehicle, its use and the type of brakes.

I have taken dimensions from my own measurements, the official SR diagrams and those provided in the various books listed in the bibliography. There are occasional variances in dimensions between the different sources. The differences are usually of little consequence to the small scale modeller. The body dimensions mean over the planking and therefore exclude fittings and overhanging roofs unless specifically noted. For modelling purposes the differences are in any case trivial. I have quoted dimensions to the nearest ½ inch, even though they may be more precisely quoted in other sources. In one instance the official diagram gives a height above rails of 8' 7 45/64". Such precision ought to be quoted at a specific ambient temperature and humidity! The height of vehicles of the same basic type varied slightly depending on whether they had timber or steel underframes. Heights are quoted to the top of the roof and exclude chimneys or ventilators. Similar vehicles varied in length depending on whether they were fitted or unfitted. Scale drawings have been prepared from these data. Some drawings have kindly been provided by colleagues, to whom I am most grateful.

I have chosen to include only those wagons that still existed in the 1960s, but which were built at any time from pre-grouping to the end of the Southern Railway. In a few instances, SR designs were adopted by BR for use in its own wagon building programme and these I have also included. Although wagons have been scrapped in their thousands, it is still possible to find examples on heritage railways. It is thus possible to select from this book wagons that would be appropriate on layouts representing any period from the early 1900s to the present day. Examples are included of typical everyday vehicles and a small number of interesting but unusual wagons and vans to add variety to a model railway.

To further assist with the choice of wagons and vans, I have included some photographs of goods and passenger van trains, from which several points are apparent. Firstly, not all goods trains were long. Many goods trains consisted of just a few wagons, a help in deciding how much stock to acquire on a layout of restricted size. Secondly, goods trains of mixed vehicles or of one particular type of vehicle were both frequently seen. It was commonplace to see a whole train of cattle or container wagons.

The origin of a wagon or van is sometimes difficult to ascertain, as in many cases repairs or rebuilds have resulted in loss of building plates. Some vehicles were sold and records of the original numbers were not always recorded. For example, the Port of Bristol Authority bought numerous wagons from the SR and some of these are now owned by heritage railways, which have had to make reasoned guesses regarding origins. Axleboxes often had the railway company initials on the castings, but over the years these were sometimes changed. For example there are wagons of SECR origin with LBSCR and SR axlebox covers, even on the same wagon. The SR often reused component parts from withdrawn vehicles to produce "new" stock or to patch up existing stock. The detail for vehicles of a given diagram number therefore changed over the years. Within a single diagram, vehicles were found with spoked or disc wheels. Some vehicles were converted for alternative uses, usually with new diagram numbers. The SR converted some of its LSWR brake vans from single to double veranda vehicles. It later converted some LBSCR and SECR brake vans from double to single veranda vehicles. At first sight this seems to be pointless, but there were at the time good reasons for such actions.

I have arranged this book by type of vehicle, rather than by railway company, in the hope that this will aid the reader in better selecting models to suit his/her purposes. Within this framework, I have arranged the vehicles in chronological order of building for each constituent company. I have quoted the SR diagram number for each vehicle. Although this is in itself of no consequence to the modeller, it will help in cases where the modeller seeks more information using the historical books referred to above. It is apparent that vehicles of the same official diagram number can be visually significantly different. The most obvious example is

INTRODUCTION

the different planking arrangements on the standard SR goods vans. In contrast, vehicles with different diagram numbers were not necessarily different in external appearance or even dimensionally. Successive diagram numbers do not necessarily imply chronological progression, even within a particular type of vehicle. For example the SR goods vans to diagram 1452 were built after similar vehicles to diagram 1458.

I have used the vehicle descriptions as entered on the official SR diagrams. For each type of vehicle I have endeavoured to provide at least one photograph, a drawing and a model. Where there are several similar wagons, I have in some cases made appropriate comments in the text, rather than reproduce virtually identical photographs and drawings. For ease of interpretation, I have kept the scale drawings uncluttered and provided the basic dimensions in tabular format. Also included are the quantities built, so that the reader can see how common was the vehicle of interest. I give dates over which building took place and some examples of vehicle numbers. These include the capital stock running numbers, and whether the vehicle was transferred to Departmental or Internal User stock. For goods vehicles in BR days the running number was usually kept for the life of the vehicle. Passenger vans were renumbered by both the SR and BR. Finally, I note whether any of the vehicles in question still exist and where they may be seen. This is not an exhaustive list, but gives examples. I have not included grounded bodies. A word of caution here, as wagons are occasionally transferred from one heritage railway to another. Many of the wagons see infrequent use and may be stored in a location inaccessible to the public. This applies particularly to those yet to undergo restoration. Some wagons in the National Collection are on loan to heritage railways. For these wagons I have quoted the name of the railway. For those at the National Railway Museum, I have given the site (York or Shildon).

Under the SR, each type of vehicle was allocated a block of numbers. For example, goods brake vans were required to be numbered between 54501 and 56999. The majority of vehicles transferred from the mainland to the Isle of Wight were renumbered into a separate series. The SR also reused the running numbers from withdrawn stock, particularly on the Isle of Wight. Vehicles subjected to a change of use (for example, open goods to loco coal) were also renumbered. Following Nationalisation, all capital vehicles were given the prefix "S". Some vehicles of SR design were built by BR and these carried the prefix "B".

From 1951 passenger rated stock received both prefix and suffix letters. The prefix denoted the owning Region and the suffix the origin of the vehicle. The vast majority of vehicles were thus numbered "SxxxxS", where "xxxx" was the former SR running number. Passenger vehicles transferred, for example, to the Western Region were renumbered "WxxxxS".

Vehicles built for or transferred to the Engineer's Department displayed the letters "ED" in SR days, replaced by the prefix "DS" (meaning Departmental Southern) in BR days. Vehicles transferred to other service use (for example, Signals and Telecommunications) were usually renumbered and given the suffix "s" in SR days and prefix "DS" in BR days. From 1970, Southern service stock was included in a new DB 975xxx series, later including a prefix indicating the department. For example "A" referred to the Mechanical and Electrical Engineers. Existing Departmental vehicles were not renumbered, although additional prefixes were added. A few vehicles were restricted to particular locations, such as a locomotive depot or goods yard (Internal Users) and starting in the 1950s, these were numbered in the series "08xxxx" for the Southern Region ("06xxxx" for the Western Region).

Where a vehicle has a suffix "s" under "Departmental Numbers" in the following pages, it is known to have been in Departmental use prior to Nationalisation. Where a prefix includes "DS", it was taken into Departmental use after Nationalisation, as far as can be ascertained. Where a vehicle is known to have been in Departmental use both prior to and following Nationalisation, I have added the suffix "s" in parenthesis to the "DS" number. The running numbers of scrapped Departmental vehicles were sometimes reissued to new acquisitions.

Quantities quoted of a particular type of vehicle at Nationalisation include both capital and Departmental stock. I have entered "not known" in instances where I have not been able to ascertain whether any of the vehicles in question still exist. This uncertainty arises because the various databases that I have consulted are incomplete, and because a few railway companies have chosen not to provide any information on their rolling stock.

It is possible to give only a summary of typical liveries and the reader is referred to the bibliography. There were many exceptions to standard liveries, and colours varied through weathering and the effects of dirt and grime. In general, vehicles were repainted as necessary, irrespective of when a new livery had been introduced. An interesting contrast to present day practice, when passenger stock is repainted every time it is leased to another train operating company.

The vast majority of goods vehicles in SR days

A PICTORIAL GUIDE TO SOUTHERN WAGONS AND VANS

were painted dark ("plain" chocolate) brown. This included the body, solebar and headstocks. Running gear and other ironware below the solebar was usually black, although on some vehicles these items were brown. Van roofs were usually grey, but some vehicles in the early years had white roofs. All lettering was white, with "S R" on the side, one letter to each side of the wagon or van door. Where space permitted the lettering was 18" high, but this was obviously not possible, for example, on flat trucks. Numbers were applied on the bottom left of vehicles and weights on the bottom right, all 5" in height. The style of lettering was changed in 1936, with "S R" near the bottom left, under which was the vehicle capacity in tons and its number, all 4" high. To the bottom right was the tare weight in the same size lettering. Lettering was reduced in size again in 1942. The same liveries were applied to containers, except those designated for furniture which were light green. Wagon sheets were usually black.

Some vehicles for special traffic, such as those for the conveyance of foodstuffs, were buff coloured, which was officially referred to as "stone". Some refrigerator vans were white. This was applied to the body and headstocks, with the solebars being black or brown. "SR", numbers and weights were in Venetian red. From 1941, red oxide was substituted for "stone". Gunpowder vans were dark brown. Brake vans had a more elaborate livery. Body sides were dark brown, but veranda ends, inside body ends and the headstocks were painted Venetian red. Ballast wagons, which one might have expected to be "stone", were in fact painted in red oxide with white lettering, as were most other engineers' vehicles. Ballast brake vans were also in red oxide, but with Venetian red ends. Other Departmental vehicles such as tool vans were usually dark grey, although some retained their capital stock livery.

Following Nationalisation, the livery adopted for unfitted vehicles was light grey. Lettering was white on a black background. Fitted vehicles (including banana vans) were painted in bauxite (red/brown), with white lettering. This was an interesting choice of colour, as it is not dissimilar to rust, particularly on dirty vehicles. Refrigerated and insulated vans were initially white with black lettering, but changed to mid blue with white lettering. Some meat vans were "stone", later some were crimson lake. For all these types of vehicle, solebars and headstocks were either black or the body colour. Other underframe components were black. Containers continued to follow the same pattern. Engineers' vehicles were painted black with yellow lettering, in later years some (including brake vans) being in olive green and more recently in grey and yellow.

SR passenger rated vehicles (including special cattle vans) were painted in the same basic livery as passenger coaches, but were not lined. This was olive green sides with black ends and underframes in the period up to 1938. Roofs were white, later changed to grey. "Southern Railway" appeared in full in the centre of the van at cantrail level in gold. The vehicle number was repeated on both the left and right of each side of the body, also in gold. Other lettering was usually in yellow. After 1938, malachite green with yellow lettering was used. During the War many vans were painted grey. The only vans to be black all over were those that had plastic bodies, built toward the end of the War. Milk tanks were painted in the colours of the company concerned, for example Express Dairies were in cobalt blue. All had black underframes, with white lettering.

Following Nationalisation, passenger vans were painted in crimson lake, about ten years later reverting to green. The final change was to rail blue. The SR Post Office vans retained green livery until the final years of their operating life, when they were painted rail blue and grey. Most milk tanks were grey or "silver" in later years.

All the models illustrated are my own, constructed in the 1970s mostly with scratch built bodies on modified proprietary underframes where available. For a few of the vehicles I have used kits or ready to run models, adapted where necessary to give a good, if not entirely accurate, representation of the prototype vehicle. All the models have been built to run and therefore the couplings are not at all true to the prototype. To give a good representation of real life, some of the models (particularly the goods stock) have been made to look dirty. Some even have peeling paint. Most of the models are in pre-War liveries, although I have included a few from a later period, or in ex Works condition.

A major difference in viewing a prototype vehicle and a model is the height and angle at which they are normally seen. A prototype vehicle is normally viewed between five and six feet from and parallel with the ground, whereas a model is viewed from a much higher perspective. It is for this reason that, where it is important, I have included photographs of roof detail.

It is inevitable in a short work of this nature, that generalisations have to be made. I hope, nevertheless, that the reader finds this book both interesting and useful.

Terry Gough
Sherborne
August 2007

ACKNOWLEDGMENTS

I am most grateful to colleagues who have contributed material for this book. In particular I thank Gerry Bixley, Mike King, Gordon Weddell, Glen Woods and the late John Smith. Thanks are also due to Roger Marsh and Colin Pattle for their help. British Railways, in its different forms, is thanked for granting permission to enter its goods yards and other premises not open to the public. I also thank the several heritage railways and museums who have provided information or given access to their Southern stock not normally on public view. Especial thanks go to Bob Allen (Mid Hants Railway), Peter Barry (Embsay & Bolton Abbey Railway), Richard Drewitt (Gloucestershire Warwickshire Steam Railway), Jerry Hawley (North Yorkshire Moors Railway), Mike Haynes (West Somerset Railway), Martin James (Swanage Railway), John Jolly (Mangapps Railway), John Miller (Yeovil Railway Centre) and Nick Tinsley (Great Central Railway).

Within my own family I thank my sister Joy, who prepared several of the drawings over 35 years ago and long before she was "renumbered" Sister Mary Julian. I also record gratitude to my wife Cynthia, who at last can see why it was necessary for me to spend so much time in Woking Yard, rather than attending to domestic affairs.

BIBLIOGRAPHY

Bixley, G, Blackburn, A, Chorley, R, King, M and Newton, J, *An Illustrated History of Southern Wagons, Volume 1* (OPC 1984: ISBN 0860932079)

Bixley, G, Blackburn, A, Chorley, R and King, M, *An Illustrated History of Southern Wagons, Volume 2* (OPC 1985: ISBN 0860932206)

Bixley, G, Blackburn, A, Chorley, R and King, M, *An Illustrated History of Southern Wagons, Volume 3* (OPC 2004: ISBN 0860934934)

Bixley, G, Blackburn, A, Chorley, R and King, M, *An Illustrated History of Southern Wagons, Volume 4* (OPC 2004: ISBN 0860935647)

Butcher, R, *Departmental Coaching Stock* (SCT Publishing 1993: ISBN 1872768105)

Butcher, R, *British Rail Internal Users* (SCT Publishing 1992: ISBN 1872768091)

Cooper, P, *LBSCR Stockbook* (Runpast Publications 1990: ISBN 1870754131)

Gould, D, *Bogie Carriages of the South Eastern & Chatham Railway* (Oakwood Press 1993: ISBN 0853614555)

Gould, D, *Bulleid's SR Steam Passenger Stock* (Oakwood Press 1980)

Gould, D, *Southern Railway Passenger Vans* (Oakwood Press 1992: ISBN 0853614288)

Hall, P and Fox, P, *Preserved Coaching Stock of British Railways Part 2 – Pre-Nationalisation Stock* (Platform 5 1996: ISBN 1872524869)

Haresnape, B, *Railway Liveries, Southern Railway* (Ian Allen 1982: ISBN 0711012032)

Kidner, R W, *Service Stock of the Southern Railway* (Oakwood Press 1993: ISBN 0853614296)

King, M, *An Illustrated History of Southern Coaches* (OPC 2003: ISBN 0860935701)

Larkin, David, *Wagons of the Early British Railways Era* (Kestrel Railway Books 2006: ISBN 9780954485986)

Lloyd, J and Brown, M, *Preserved Railway Carriages* (Silver Link 1992: ISBN 0947971750)

Maycock, R J and Reed, M J E, *Isle of Wight Steam Passenger Rolling Stock* (Oakwood Press 1997: ISBN 0853615071)

Rowland, D, *British Railways Wagons* (OPC 1996: ISBN 0752903780)

Tavender, L, *HMRS Livery Register No 3, LSWR and Southern* (Historical Model Railway Society 1970: ISBN 902835009)

Weddell, G R, *LSWR Carriages Vol. 1 1838-1900* (Wild Swan Publications Ltd 1992: ISBN 1874103089)

Weddell, G R, *LSWR Carriages Vol. 3 Non Passenger Carriage Stock* (Kestrel Railway Books 2005: ISBN 0954485955)

Various heritage and other railway publications and web sites

List of Current Locations of Rolling Stock

Abbreviation	Full Name	Abbreviation	Full Name
BidefordC	Bideford Railway Heritage Centre	KESR	Kent & East Sussex Railway
BluebellR	Bluebell Railway	LlangollenR	Llangollen Railway
BodminR	Bodmin & Wenford Railway	MangappsR	Mangapps Railway
Bo'nessR	Bo'ness & Kinneil Railway	MidlandC	Midland Railway Centre
BucksR	Buckinghamshire Railway Centre	MoorsR	North Yorkshire Moors Railway
ChasewaterR	Chasewater Railway	NeneR	Nene Valley Railway
ColneR	Colne Valley Railway	PlymR	Plym Valley Railway
DartR	Paignton and Dartmouth Steam Railway	RotherR	Rother Valley Railway
		SevernR	Severn Valley Railway
DidcotC	Didcot Railway Centre	ShildonM	National Railway Museum
EKR	East Kent Railway	SpaR	Spa Valley Railway
EmbsayR	Embsay & Bolton Abbey Railway	SwanageR	Swanage Railway
ESomR	East Somerset Railway	WightR	Isle of Wight Steam Railway
GlosR	Gloucestershire Warwickshire Steam Railway	WorthR	Keighley & Worth Valley Railway
		WSomR	West Somerset Railway
GwiliR	Gwili Railway	YeovilC	Yeovil Railway Centre
HantsR	Mid Hants Railway	YorkM	National Railway Museum
IcknieldR	Chinnor & Princes Risborough Railway		

Prefixes and Suffixes to Vehicle Numbers

ADB, ADS (prefixes)	Mechanical & Electrical Engineers' Department	KDS (prefix)	Signal & Telecommunication Engineers' Department
B (prefix)	BR built vehicle	s (suffix)	Service stock
CDS (prefix)	Civil Engineers' Department (BR Engineering Ltd)	S (prefix)	Former SR capital stock vehicle
		TDB (prefix)	Traffic Department (Operating Department)
DB (prefix)	Departmental, BR		
DS (prefix)	Departmental, Southern		

Abbreviations (other)

AD	Army Department	LNER	London & North Eastern Railway
BR	British Railways	LSWR	London & South Western Railway
GWR	Great Western Railway	MoS	Ministry of Supply
IOW	Isle of Wight	SDJR	Somerset & Dorset Joint Railway
LBSCR	London, Brighton & South Coast Railway	SECR	South Eastern & Chatham Railway
LMSR	London, Midland & Scottish Railway	SR	Southern Railway

SR passenger guard's van number S392 (diagram 3093) at Bodmin Parkway on 23rd July 2005. (Terry Gough)

CHAPTER 1

GOODS VEHICLES

Open Goods and Mineral Wagons

Nothing could be simpler than a basic open wagon. Despite this, there are many variations. The most obvious feature is the number of planks from which the body sides are constructed, ranging from a single plank to eight planks. Other variations include wagons with side opening or end opening doors, round body ends, wooden or steel underframes, brake gear, vacuum fitted or not. Within each of the versions there are further differences, for example whether split spoked, solid spoked or disc (solid or with three or four holes) wheels. It is not surprising therefore that each of the companies constituting the Southern Railway had open wagons to many different diagrams.

Many more open wagons of LBSCR origin survived into BR days than those of the LSWR and SECR. This is because it was LBSCR open wagons that had been transferred to the Isle of Wight decades previously, in preference to wagons of the other companies. The number of miles these wagons travelled on the Island was far less than wagons on the Mainland, and they therefore survived for much longer. The expense of transferring wagons from the Mainland also mitigated against replacements until absolutely necessary. A few vehicles of LSWR, SECR and SR origin did however reach the Island and these too survived until the end of steam operation.

An assortment of pre-grouping wagons at Newport IOW on 20th September 1965. The open wagons are mostly of LBSCR and Isle of Wight Railway origin. The brake vans were all from the LSWR and the goods train is being hauled by LSWR Class O2 No 21 Sandown. (Terry Gough)

A PICTORIAL GUIDE TO SOUTHERN WAGONS AND VANS

SECR 4-plank dropside open goods wagon

Built by or for	SECR
SR diagram number	1352
Description	10-ton 4-plank dropside open goods wagon
Quantity purchased	100
Approx quantity at Nationalisation	20
Dates (purchased second-hand)	1901/2
Underframe material	timber
Wheelbase	9' 0"
Body length	15' 0"
Overall length	18' 0"
Body width	7' 6"
Height above rails	6' 4½"
SR running numbers (examples)	14781 – 14841, IOW 62885 – 62904
Departmental numbers (examples)	DS62888, DS62896
Internal user numbers	none known
Examples extant	62888
Location	WightR

A total of twenty of these wagons were transferred to the Isle of Wight in 1924 and 1931, where they were rebuilt and renumbered. They were by far the longest surviving SECR open wagons and lasted in BR ownership until 1967.

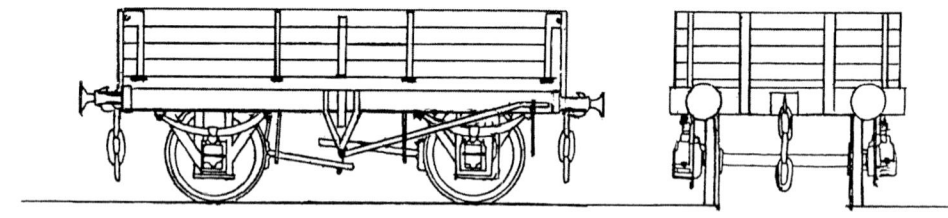

SECR 4-plank dropside open goods wagon (diagram 1352). (Terry Gough)

SECR 4-plank dropside open goods wagon number DS62896 photographed at Newport IOW on 10th August 1965. (Terry Gough)

OPEN GOODS AND MINERAL WAGONS

*SECR 4-plank dropside open goods wagon number DS62890 photographed at Sandown on 14th August 1966.
(Terry Gough)*

LBSCR 5-plank open goods wagon

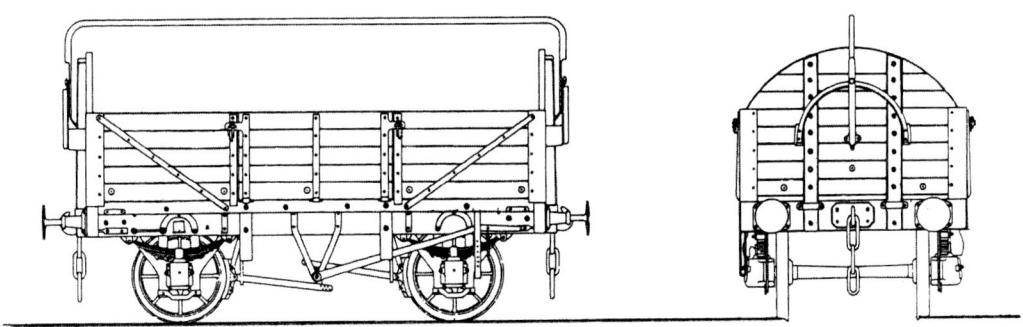

*LBSCR 5-plank open goods wagon (diagram 1369).
(Gerry Bixley)*

*LBSCR 5-plank open goods wagon number S28277 photographed at Medina Wharf on 12th August 1965.
(Terry Gough)*

A PICTORIAL GUIDE TO SOUTHERN WAGONS AND VANS

Company	LBSCR
SR diagram number	1369
Description	10-ton 5-plank open goods wagon
Approximate quantity built	3,500
Dates	1905 – 1926
Approx. quantity at Nationalisation	1,400
Underframe material	timber
Wheelbase	9' 3"
Body length	15' 5"
Overall length	18' 5"
Body width	7' 9"
Height above rails	7' 0"
SR running numbers (examples)	18729 – 19078, IOW 28253 – 28300
Departmental numbers (examples)	189s ex 18769, DS64396 ex 28346
Internal user numbers	none known
Examples extant	LBSCR 3346 27730 27884
Location	BluebellR WightR YeovilC

Wagons built to this diagram were the most numerous of all LBSCR open wagons.
The earliest wagons to this diagram were built with rounded ends, making the end height above rails 9' 0".
Some of the round ended wagons were converted by the SR to square ended and given diagram No 1364. The majority of vehicles were built with square ends. Some were converted to dropside wagons.
Between 1924 and 1931, 450 wagons were transferred to the Isle of Wight.

LBSCR 5-plank open goods wagon number S28352 photographed at Medina Wharf on 12th August 1965. (Terry Gough)

LBSCR 5-plank open goods wagon number 3346 photographed at Horsted Keynes on 24th June 1996. (Terry Gough)

OPEN GOODS AND MINERAL WAGONS

SR 8-plank open goods wagon

Built by or for	SR
SR diagram number	1379
Description	12- or 13-ton 8-plank open goods wagon
Quantity built	7,950
Dates	1926 – 1933
Approx. quantity at Nationalisation	7,000
Underframe material	steel
Wheelbase	9' 0"
Body length	17' 6"
Overall length	20' 6"
Body width	7' 11"
Height above rails	8' 7½"
SR running numbers	29001 – 35150
Departmental numbers (example)	DS29487 as diagram 1378
Internal user numbers	none known
Examples extant	none known

This was the most numerous of any SR designed open wagon. Some were converted to carry cable drums and given diagram number 1378 or 1899.

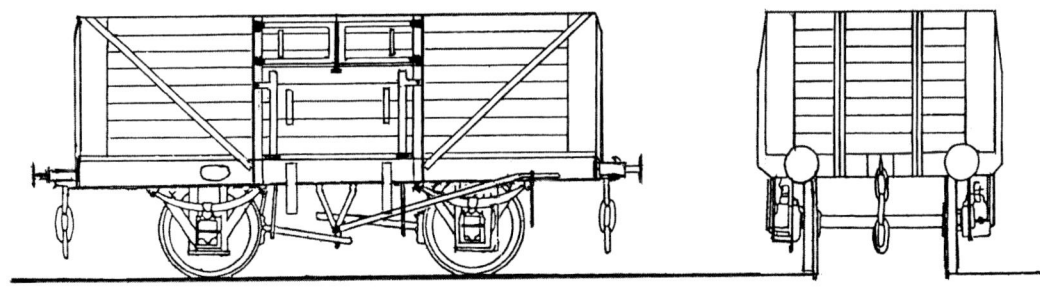

SR 8-plank open goods wagon (diagram 1379). (Terry Gough)

SR 8-plank open goods wagon number S34301 photographed at Worcester on 14th August 1966. (Terry Gough)

A PICTORIAL GUIDE TO SOUTHERN WAGONS AND VANS

SR 8-plank open goods wagon number DS29487 photographed at Micheldever on 27th May 1969. (Terry Gough)

SR 8-plank mineral wagon

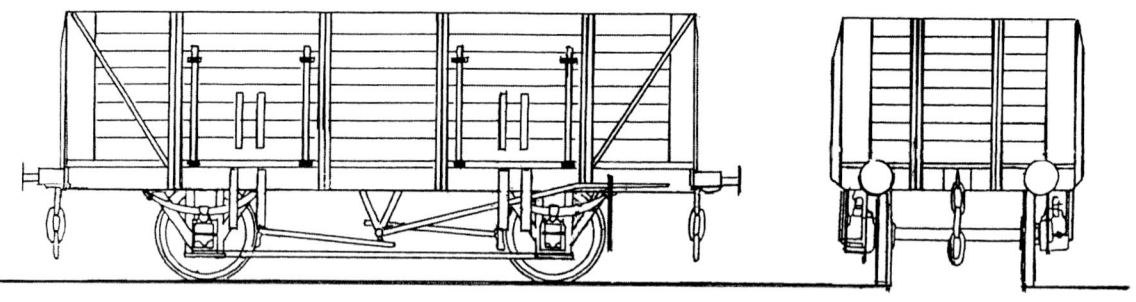

SR 8-plank mineral wagon (diagram 1386). (Terry Gough)

SR 8-plank mineral wagon number S40434. (John Smith)

OPEN GOODS AND MINERAL WAGONS

Built by or for	SR
SR diagram number	1386
Description	20-ton or 21-ton 8-plank mineral wagon
Approximate quantity built	1,000
Dates	1933 – 1939
Approx. quantity at Nationalisation	1,000
Underframe material	steel
Wheelbase	12' 0"
Body length	21' 6"
Overall length	24' 6"
Body width	8' 0"
Height above rails	9' 0"
SR running numbers	40201 – 40980
Departmental numbers	DS70185 ex 40224
Internal user numbers	none known
Examples extant	none known

These wagons are shown as 9-plank on the official diagram.

SR 8-plank open goods wagon

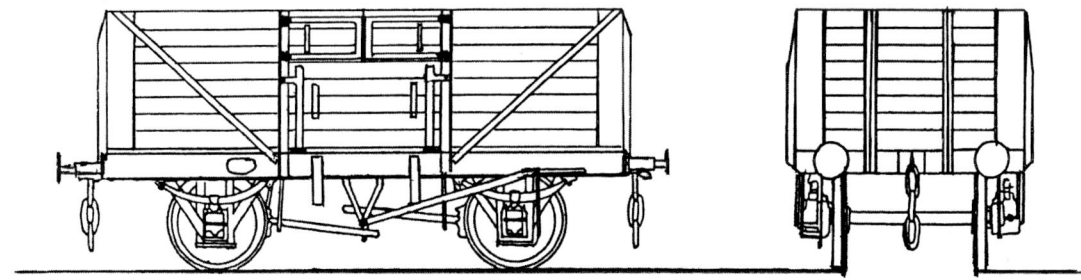

SR 8-plank open goods wagon (diagram 1400). (Terry Gough)

SR 8-plank open goods wagon number S26779 photographed at Woking on 27th May 1969. (Terry Gough)

7

A PICTORIAL GUIDE TO SOUTHERN WAGONS AND VANS

Built by or for	SR
SR diagram number	1400
Description	10-ton or 13-ton 8-plank open goods wagon
Approximate quantity built	1,400
Dates	1936 – 1939
Approx. quantity at Nationalisation	1,400
Underframe material	steel
Wheelbase	10' 0"
Body length	17' 6"
Overall length	20' 6"
Body width	7' 11"
Height above rails	8' 8"
SR running numbers	26719 – 26901
Departmental numbers	none known
Internal user numbers	none known
Example extant	11093
Location	MangappsR

Many converted to vacuum brakes by BR.

SR 8-plank open goods wagon number S11093 photographed at Burnham on Crouch on 23rd November 2005. (Terry Gough)

SR 5-plank open goods wagon

Built by or for	SR/MoS/LNER/BR	BR
SR diagram number	1375	1/034
Description	13-ton 5-plank open goods wagon	
Approximate quantity built	3,000	600
Dates	1940 – 1948	1949/50
Approx. quantity at Nationalisation	2,800	
Underframe material	steel	steel
Wheelbase	10' 0"	10' 0"
Body length	17' 6"	17' 6"
Overall length	20' 6"	20' 6"
Body width	8' 0"	8' 0"
Height above rails	7' 3"	7' 3"
Running numbers (examples)	5400 – 5572	B477050 – 477649
Departmental numbers	none known	none known
Internal user numbers	060798 ex 38222	
Example extant	5869	
Location	NeneR	

Many were fitted with vacuum brakes.

8

OPEN GOODS AND MINERAL WAGONS

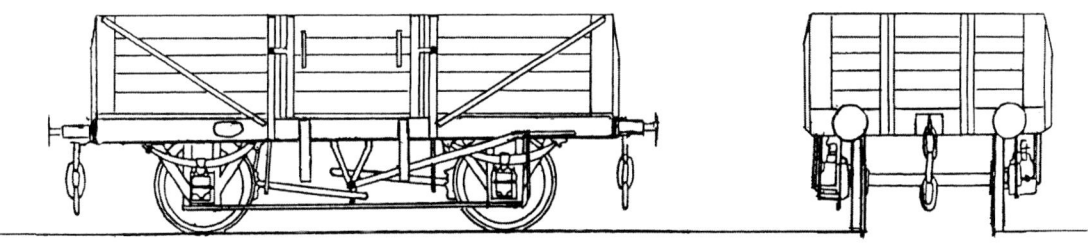
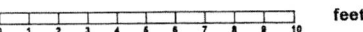

SR 5-plank open goods wagon (diagram 1375). (Terry Gough)

Above: SR 5-plank open goods wagon number S5508 photographed at Woking on 8th March 1969. (Terry Gough)

Left: Model of an SR 5-plank open goods wagon. (Terry Gough)

SR/BR 5-plank shock-absorbing open goods wagon

Built by or for	SR/BR	BR
SR diagram number	1392	1/035
Description	12/13-ton 5-plank open goods wagon, shock absorbing	
Quantity built	38	800
Dates	1949	1950
Underframe material	steel	steel
Wheelbase	10' 0"	10' 0"
Body length	16' 6"	16' 6"
Length over headstocks	17' 6"	17' 6"
Overall length	20' 6"	20' 6"
Body width	8' 0"	8' 0"
Height above rails	7' 8"	7' 8"
Running numbers (examples)	14033 – 14070	B720425 – 721224
Departmental numbers	none known	none known
Internal user numbers	none known	none known
Example extant	14036	none known
Location	MoorsR	

Shock-absorbing wagons to diagram 1376 (Nos 38395 – 38400) were almost identical.

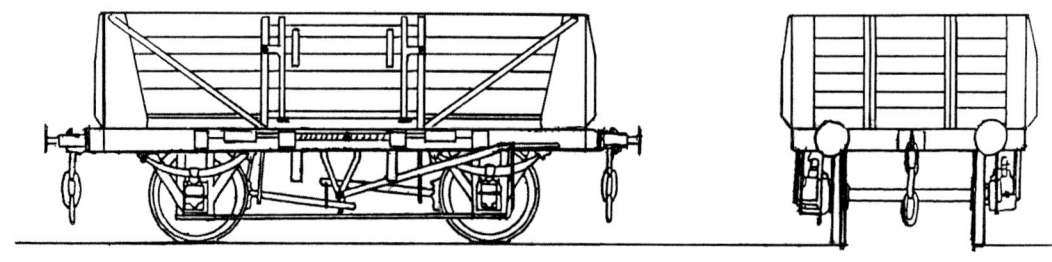

SR/BR 5-plank shock-absorbing open goods wagon (diagram 1392). (Terry Gough)

SR/BR 5-plank shock-absorbing open goods wagon number S14036 photographed at Goathland on 29th June 2006. (Terry Gough)

Covered Goods Wagons

A typical pick up goods train with a miscellaneous collection of wagons from different railway companies is seen at Uckfield on 27th March 1961. The first vehicle is one of the most common SR vans, seen all over the country. The engine is ex LBSCR Class K No 32339. (Terry Gough)

There was a Fyffe's banana depot at Kingston and on 2nd August 1962 SR Class W No 31924 pauses between shunting. The last vehicle is an SR banana van to diagram 1478. To the right of the engine is SR brake van No S55972 to diagram 1578. (Terry Gough)

A PICTORIAL GUIDE TO SOUTHERN WAGONS AND VANS

LSWR covered goods wagon

Built by or for	LSWR
SR diagram number	1410
Description	10-ton covered goods wagon
Approximate quantity built	1,000
Dates	1885 – 1912
Quantity at Nationalisation	260
Underframe material	timber or steel
Wheelbase	10' 6"
Body length	18' 0"
Overall length	21' 0"
Body width	7' 9½"
Height above rails	11' 0½" steel
SR running numbers (examples)	43930 – 44106
Departmental numbers (examples)	DS43161, DS43405, DS554 ex 44124
Internal user number (example)	080133 ex 42455
Example extant	2773 (LSWR No)
Location	BluebellR

These are very similar to the ventilated wagons of diagrams 1401/2, but were for general traffic, and were fitted with only a single ventilation cover at each end. The end window on DS43161 in the photograph is an addition for Departmental use. Note the different brake gear in the two photographs.

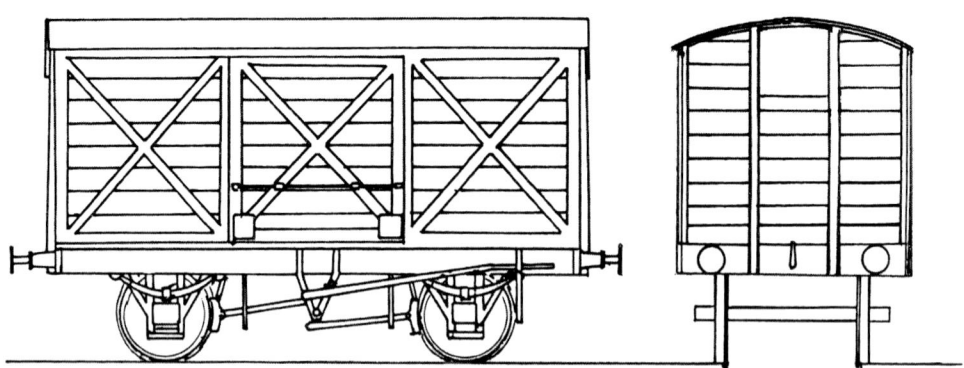

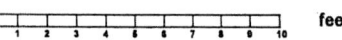

LSWR covered goods wagon (diagram 1410). (Joy Gough)

Model of LSWR covered goods wagon number 42601. (Terry Gough)

12

COVERED GOODS WAGONS

LSWR covered goods wagon number DS43405 photographed at Guildford on 30th December 1966. (Terry Gough)

LSWR covered goods wagon number DS43161 photographed at Eastleigh on 9th August 1966. (Terry Gough)

A PICTORIAL GUIDE TO SOUTHERN WAGONS AND VANS

LSWR ventilated covered goods wagons

Built by or for	LSWR	
SR diagram number	1401	1402
Description	8-ton ventilated covered goods wagon	8- and 10-ton ventilated covered goods wagon
Quantity built	150	23
Dates	1908 – 1910	1887 – 1906
Quantity at Nationalisation	unknown	8
Underframe material	timber	timber or steel
Wheelbase	11' 0"	10' 6"
Body length	18' 0"	18' 0"
Overall length	21' 5"	21' 0"
Body width	7' 9½"	7' 9½"
Height above rails	11' 1½"	11' 0½"
Running numbers (examples)	42001 – 42139 (mixed 1401 and 1402)	
Departmental numbers	1782s ex 42052	1936s ex 42077
Internal user numbers	none known	none known
Example extant	42106	
Location	WSomR	

All were vacuum piped or braked and some were passenger rated. These had Mansell solid wheels of 3' 5" diameter and longer leaf springs. The end ventilation panels varied, some having a single ventilation cover and others a series of louvres. Some wagons had torpedo ventilators. The wagons were used for, among other commodities, fish, butter, fruit and meat.

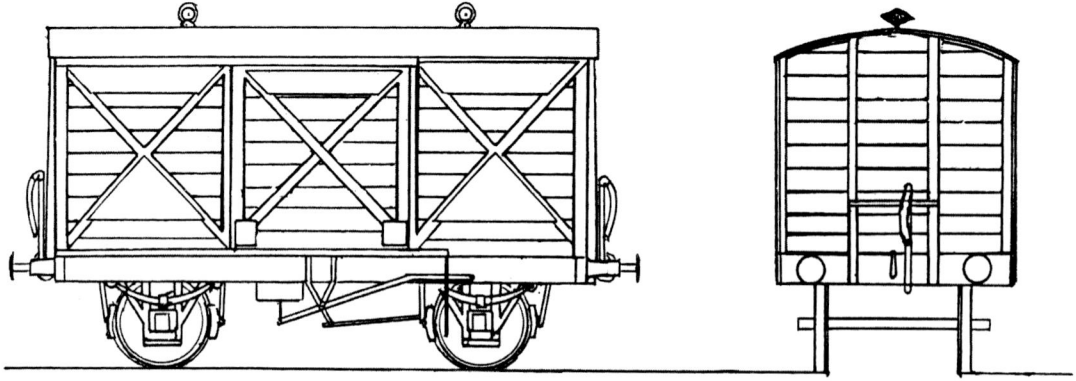

LSWR ventilated covered goods wagon (diagram 1401). (Terry Gough)

LSWR ventilated covered goods wagon number AD47763 (SR number unknown) photographed at Longmoor on 30th April 1966. (Terry Gough)

COVERED GOODS WAGONS

LSWR/SR covered goods wagon

Built by or for	LSWR	LSWR/SR
SR diagram number	1409	1408
Description	10-ton covered goods wagons	
Approximate quantity built	600	400
Dates	1912 – 1922	1916 – 1924
Approx. quantity at Nationalisation	400	500
Underframe material	timber	steel
Wheelbase	10' 6"	10' 6"
Body length	18' 0"	18' 0"
Overall length	21' 0"	21' 0"
Body width	8' 0"	8' 0"
Height above rails	11' 9"	11' 8"
SR running numbers (examples)	44110 – 44117	44276 – 44425
Departmental numbers (example)	184s ex 43192	1978s ex 43746, DS44293
Internal user numbers	none known	none known
Examples extant	none known	none known

The only significant difference between the wagons of these two diagrams is that one was on a timber underframe and the other on steel. They differ from LSWR wagons to diagram 1410 (page 12) in several respects, the most obvious being replacement of a sliding door with hinged doors.

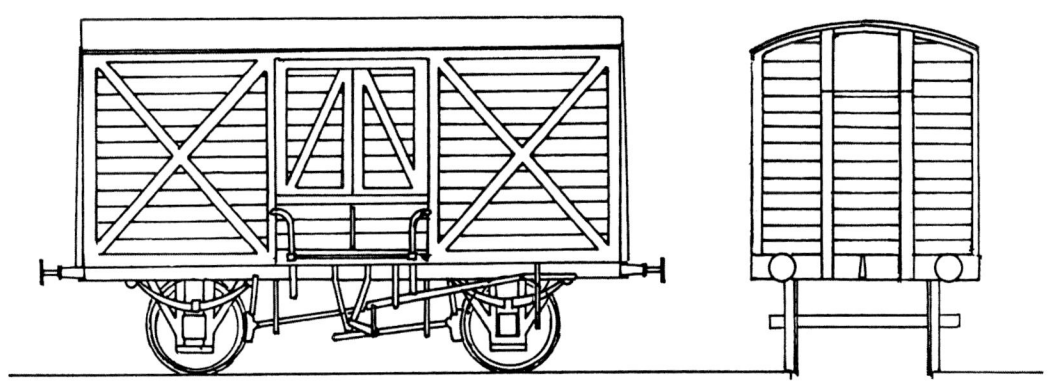

LSWR/SR covered goods wagon (diagram 1409). (Terry Gough)

LSWR/SR covered goods wagon number DS44293 photographed at Exeter Central on 3rd June 1966. (Terry Gough)

Model of LSWR/SR covered goods wagon number 44293 (diagram 1409). (Terry Gough)

LBSCR covered goods wagon

Built by or for	LBSCR	LBSCR
SR diagram number	1433 (8-ton)	1436 (10-ton)
Description	Covered goods wagon	
Quantity built	429	35
Dates	1878 – 1915	1920 – 1923
Quantity at Nationalisation	35	27
Underframe material	timber	timber
Wheelbase	9' 9"	9' 9"
Body length	18' 4"	18' 4"
Overall length	21' 4"	21' 4"
Body width	7' 8½"	7' 8½"
Height above rails	11' 3"	11' 3"
SR running numbers (examples)	46192 – 46620	46739 – 46773
	IOW 46941 – 46974 (diagrams mixed)	
Departmental numbers (examples)	1128s ex 46571, DS1374(s) ex 46281	DS1704(s) ex 46773, DS46957
Internal user number	081373	
Examples extant	46544 BluebellR	LBSCR 3713 (SR 46773) WightR unknown number Chatham Dockyard

Similar 8-ton egg and refrigeration vans were also built by the LBSCR.

Model of LBSCR covered goods wagon number 46540 (diagram 1433). (Terry Gough)

COVERED GOODS WAGONS

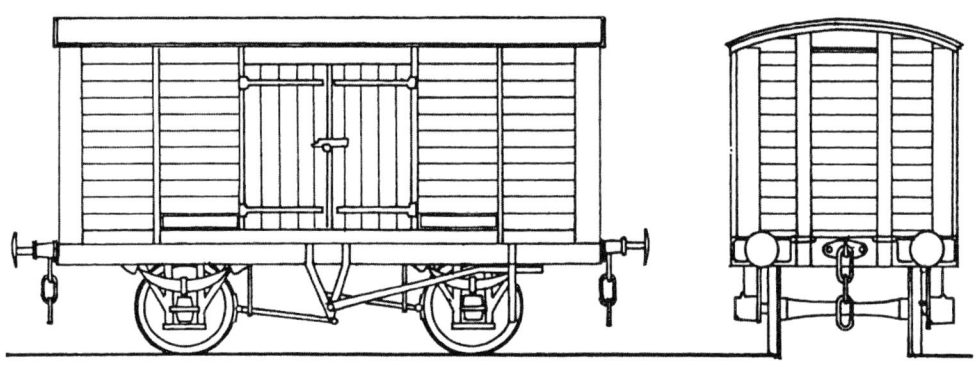

LBSCR covered goods wagon (diagram 1433). (Joy Gough)

LBSCR covered goods wagon number 081373 photographed at Newport on 12th August 1965. (Terry Gough)

LBSCR covered goods wagon number DS46957 photographed at Newport on 12th August 1965. (Terry Gough)

SECR covered goods wagon

Built by or for	SECR
SR diagram number	1425
Description	10-ton covered goods wagon
Approximate quantity built	100
Dates	1909 – 1914
Quantity at Nationalisation	4
Underframe material	timber
Wheelbase	9' 6"
Body length	17' 0"
Overall length	20' 0" unfitted, 20' 6" fitted
Body width	8' 0"
Height above rails	11' 11"
SR running numbers (examples)	45465-45561
Departmental numbers (examples)	DS1904(s) ex 45465, DS1703(s) ex 45513
Internal user numbers	none known
Examples extant	none known

Unfitted versions had spoked wheels, fitted wagons had Mansell wheels.

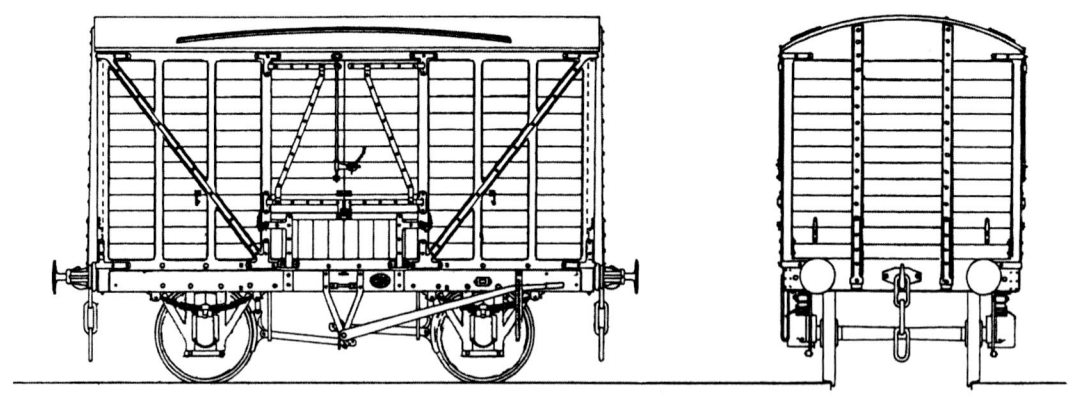

SECR covered goods wagon (diagram 1425). (Mike King)

SECR covered goods wagon number 1904s photographed at Exmouth Junction in September 1949. (John Smith)

COVERED GOODS WAGONS

SECR/SR covered goods wagon

Built by or for	SECR/SR
SR diagram number	1426
Description	10-ton covered goods wagon
Approximate quantity built	400
Dates	1915 – 1926
Approx. quantity at Nationalisation	400
Underframe material	steel
Wheelbase	9' 6"
Body length	17' 0"
Overall length	20' 0" unfitted, 20' 5" fitted
Body width	7' 10"
Height above rails	12' 3"
SR running numbers (examples)	45708 – 45907 (SECR), 47101 – 47200 (SR)
Departmental numbers (example)	DS45682, DS1921(s) ex 45683, DS45871
Internal user numbers (examples)	080429, 080434, 080697 ex 45767
Example extant	SECR 15750 (SR 45767)
Location	BluebellR

Nos 45624 – 45707 were vacuum fitted. These were the forerunner of the standard SR (Maunsell) van (see subsequent pages).

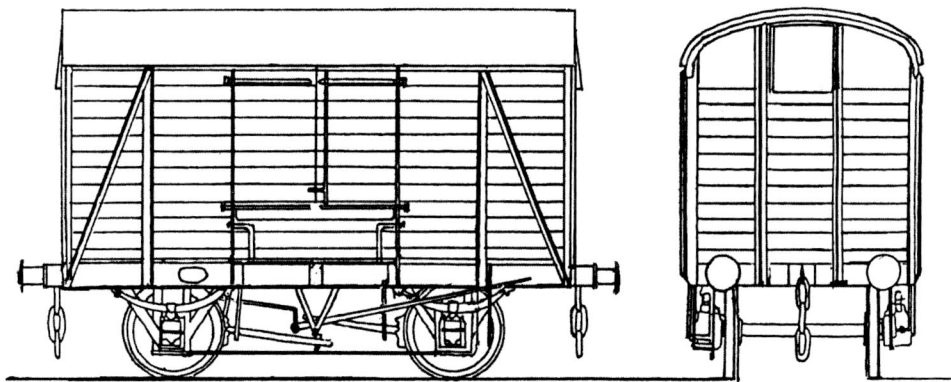

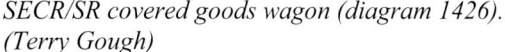

SECR/SR covered goods wagon (diagram 1426). (Terry Gough)

See also the model based on diagram 1458, illustrated on page 22.

SECR/SR covered goods wagon number DS45871 photographed post-1948, possibly at Ashford. (John Smith)

19

SR covered goods wagon

Built by or for	SR
SR diagram number	1428
Description	12-ton covered goods wagon
Approximate quantity built	1,000
Dates	1929 – 1935
Approx. quantity at Nationalisation	1,000
Underframe material	steel
Wheelbase	9' 0"
Body length	17' 6"
Overall length	20' 6" unfitted, 20' 11" fitted
Body width	7' 10"
Height above rails	12' 3"
SR running numbers (example)	47201 – 47550
Departmental numbers (example)	DS47229, DS1839(s) ex 47895
Internal user numbers (example)	081973 ex 44656 (diagram 1429), 082048 ex 47588
Examples extant	47588 44010?
Location	BluebellR BidefordC

These wagons were developed from diagram 1426 (page 19) and thousands were ultimately built with minor variations and different diagram numbers, for example 1429, 1452, 1455, 1458, 1479. Some examples are on the following pages. There were both fitted and unfitted versions.

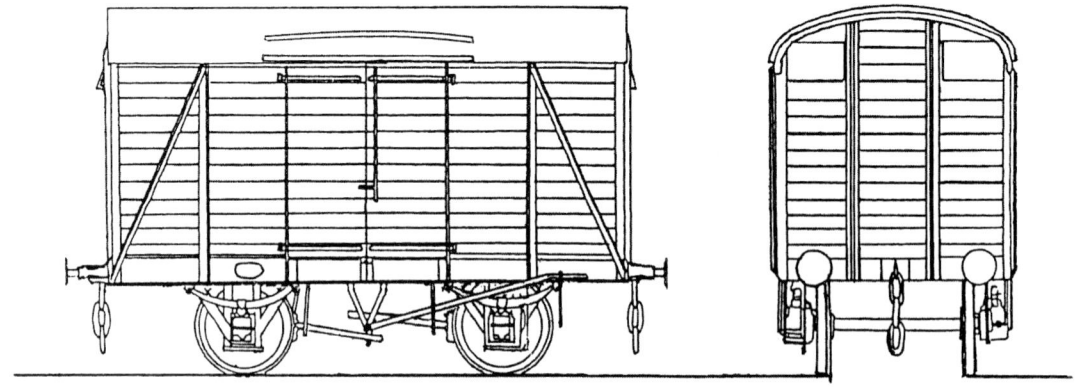

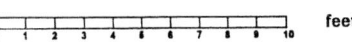

SR covered goods wagon (diagram 1428). (Terry Gough)

See also the model based on diagram 1458, illustrated on page 22.

SR covered goods wagon number DS47229 photographed at Guildford in February 1967. (Terry Gough)

COVERED GOODS WAGONS

SR covered goods wagon

Built by or for	SR
SR diagram number	1458
Description	12-ton covered goods wagon
Approximate quantity built	3,000
Dates	1936 – 1941
Quantity at Nationalisation	all
Underframe material	steel
Wheelbase	10' 0"
Body length	17' 6"
Overall length	20' 11"
Body width	8' 4½"
Height above rails	12' 3"
SR running numbers (examples)	48277 – 48776, 59251 – 60000
Departmental numbers (examples)	DS1729(s) ex 48491, DS48564, CDS1817 ex 48852
Internal user numbers (examples)	083489 ex ADS48564, 083507 ex 48852, 064821 ex 59524
Examples extant	48949 49445
Location	WSomR ?

This has obviously been developed from the SECR design. Despite being to the same diagram, the two vehicles illustrated are obviously different. The vehicle shown on page 22 has a body constructed of equal width planks, whereas the body of the vehicle shown on this page consists of alternate pairs of wide and narrow planks. All wagons were fitted.

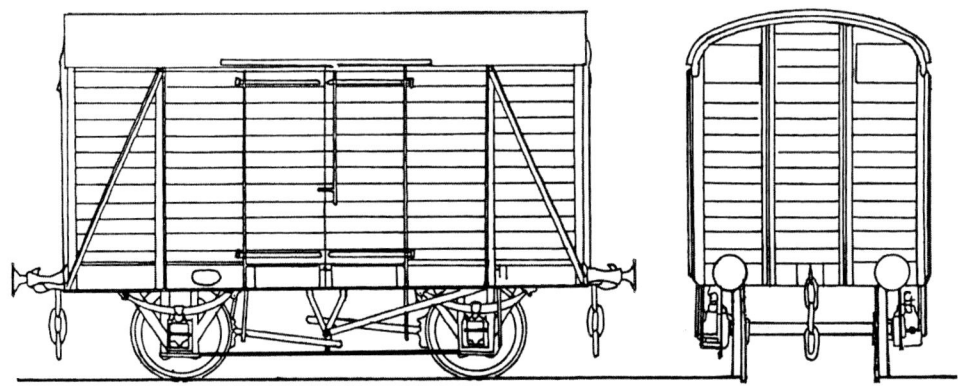

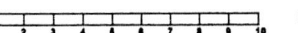

SR covered goods wagon (diagram 1458). (Joy Gough)

SR covered goods wagon number S59262 photographed at Wymondham on 3rd October 1968. (Terry Gough)

21

A PICTORIAL GUIDE TO SOUTHERN WAGONS AND VANS

Above and right: SR covered goods wagon number DS48564 photographed at Woking on 31st August 1968. Note the odd axlebox covers.
(Terry Gough)

Model of SR covered goods wagon number 48551 (diagram 1458).
(Terry Gough)

COVERED GOODS WAGONS

SR/BR covered goods wagon

Built by or for	SR/LMSR/GWR	SR/BR
SR diagram number	1455	1452, 1/202
Description	12-ton covered goods wagon	
Approximate quantity built	2,800	1,800
Dates	1942 – 1944	1945 – 1949
Quantity at Nationalisation	1,800 (that is, all for SR)	1053 (that is, all)
Underframe material	steel	steel
Wheelbase	10' 0"	10' 0"
Body length	17' 6"	17' 6"
Overall length	20' 6"	20' 6"
Body width	8' 4½" over roof	8' 4½" over roof
Height above rails	12' 3"	12' 3"
SR running numbers (example)	65281 – 65979	56501 – 57010, B752350 – 753099
Departmental number (example)	DS1842(s) ex 49393	none known
Internal user numbers	none known	none known
Examples extant	none known	none known

The van illustrated below has presumably been repaired at some stage, as the planking on the top left is different to remainder of the body. The van illustrated at the bottom of page 24 is the plywood bodied version of diagram 1455. The position of the end ventilators varied, some being a single central high level cover.

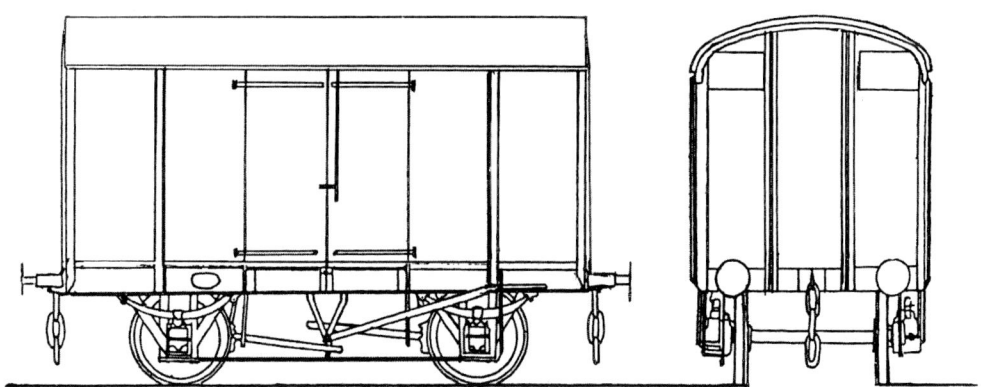

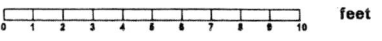

SR/BR covered goods wagon (diagram 1452). (Terry Gough)

SR/BR covered goods wagon number S65469 photographed at Woking in June 1966. (Terry Gough)

See also the model based on diagram 1458, illustrated on page 22.

SR/BR covered goods wagon number S56501 photographed at Wymondham on 30th October 1968. (Terry Gough)

Detail from SR/BR covered goods wagon number S56501 photographed at Wymondham on 30th October 1968. (Terry Gough)

SR/BR covered goods wagon number B753047 photographed at Clapham Junction on 13th August 1968. This is the plywood bodied version of diagram 1455. (Terry Gough)

COVERED GOODS WAGONS

SR banana van

Built by or for	SR
SR diagram number	1478
Description	10-ton banana van
Quantity built	200
Date	1935
Quantity at Nationalisation	all
Underframe material	steel
Wheelbase	10' 0"
Body length	17' 6"
Overall length	20' 11"
Body width	8' 0"
Height above rails	12' 2½"
SR running numbers	50575 – 50774
Departmental numbers	none
Internal user numbers	none
Examples extant	none

All vans were vacuum fitted. See page 11 for another photograph of a banana van.

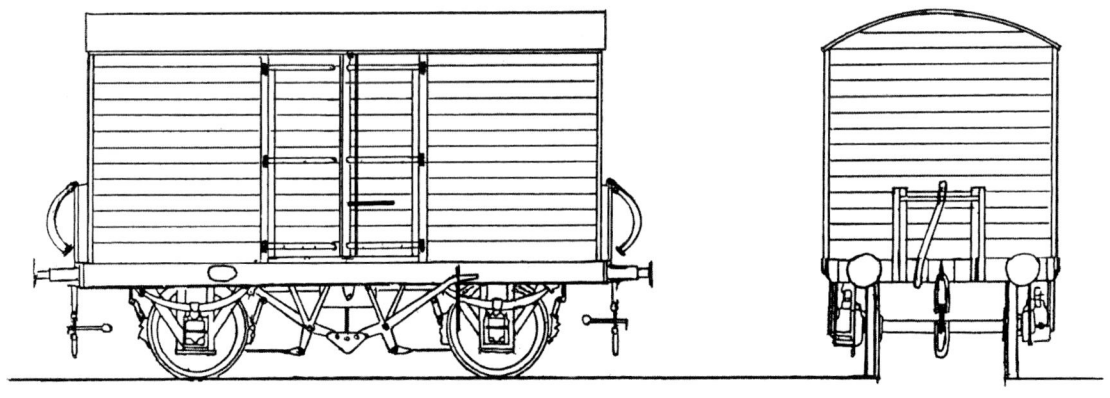

SR banana van (diagram 1478). (Terry Gough)

Model of SR banana van number 50746 (diagram 1478). (Terry Gough)

SR banana van number 50746 photographed pre-1948 at an unknown location. (CJ Binnie courtesy of John Smith)

SR banana van

Built by or for	SR
SR diagram number	1479
Description	10-ton banana van
Quantity built	125
Date	1938
Quantity at Nationalisation	all
Underframe material	steel
Wheelbase	10' 0"
Body length	17' 6"
Overall length	20' 11"
Body width	8' 4½"
Height above rails	12' 3"
SR running numbers	50775 – 50899
Departmental numbers	none known
Internal user numbers	none known
Examples extant	none known

This was virtually a standard SR goods wagon (diagram 1458 on page 21), but without the end ventilators. All were vacuum fitted. See also the model of 1458 illustrated on page 22.

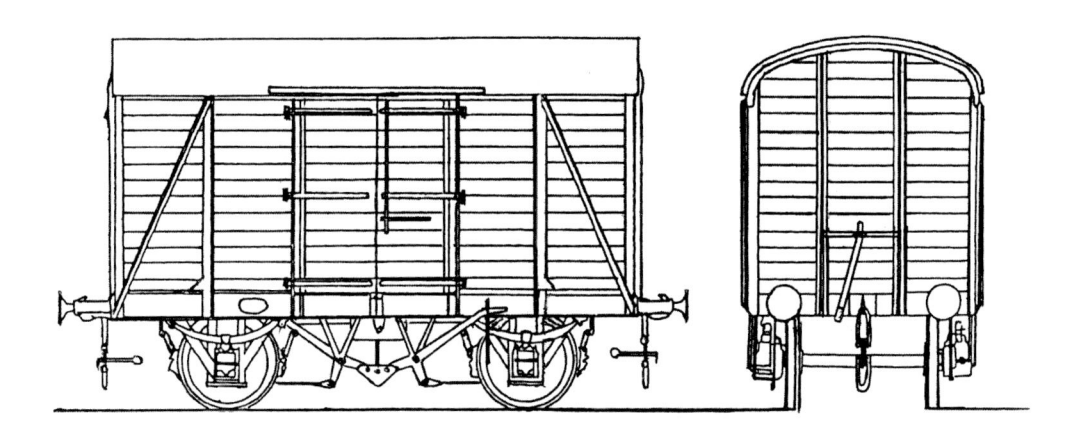

COVERED GOODS WAGONS

SR banana van (diagram 1479). (Terry Gough)

SR banana van number S50810 photographed at Micheldever in the 1960s. (John Smith)

A PICTORIAL GUIDE TO SOUTHERN WAGONS AND VANS
Cattle Wagons and Special Cattle Vans

A train of cattle wagons approaches Woking on 20th November 1962. The second wagon from the front of the train is an SR cattle wagon to diagram 1529. Cattle wagons were a common sight across the country, but the decision by the railways to stop transporting cattle resulted in the wagons being scrapped in thousands over a very short period. Since they were of little use for Departmental purposes, hardly any have survived. (Terry Gough)

Vehicles not fitted for push pull operation were attached to the rear of trains being propelled, such as on the 10.19am from Horsham to Brighton, seen at Christ's Hospital on 24th March 1960. The cattle wagon B893147 is to BR diagram 3/153, which unfortunately is only superficially similar to SR cattle wagons of diagram 1529. SR cattle wagons were distinctive in that the diagonal body struts ran from the headstocks toward the upper part of the doors, rather than the other way round. (Terry Gough)

CATTLE WAGONS AND SPECIAL CATTLE VANS

LSWR large cattle wagon

Built by or for	LSWR
SR diagram number	1501, 1502
Description	8-ton large cattle wagon
Quantity built	250
Date	1911 – 1923
Quantity at Nationalisation	46
Underframe material	timber
Wheelbase	11' 0"
Body length	18' 8½"
Overall length	22' 1½"
Body width	8' 2"
Height above rails	11' 8"
SR running numbers (examples)	51803 – 51816
Departmental numbers	none
Internal user numbers	none
Examples extant	none

Wagons to diagrams 1501 and 1502 were externally identical. Mansell wheels of 3' 5" diameter were fitted.

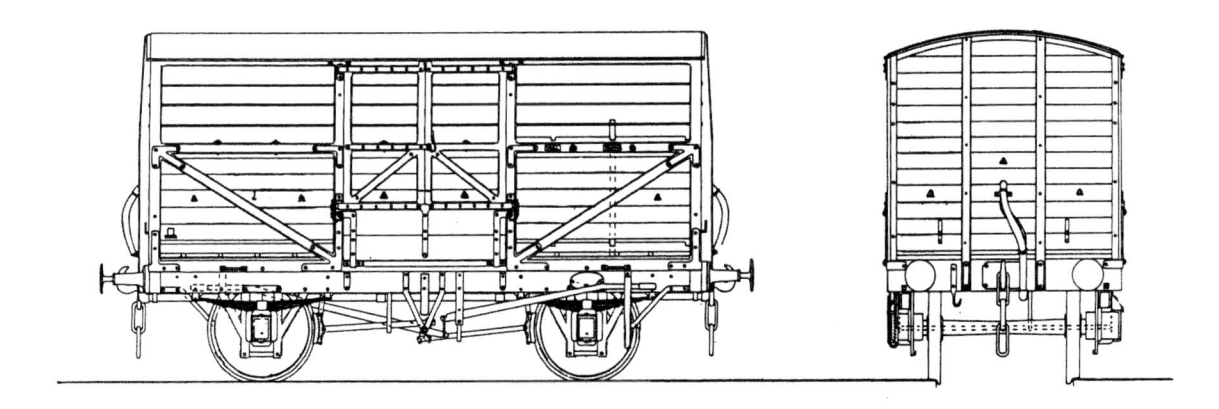

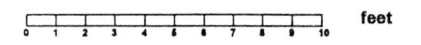

LSWR large cattle wagon (diagram 1501, 1502). (Mike King)

LSWR large cattle wagon number S51745. (British Railways)

SECR special cattle van

Built by or for	SECR
SR diagram number	1051
Description	7- and 8-ton special cattle van
Quantity built	13
Date	1922
Quantity at Nationalisation	7
Underframe material	timber
Wheelbase	10' 6"
Body length	19' 0"
Overall length	22' 6"
Body width	8' 1"
Height above rails	11' 4"
SR running numbers (examples)	3746 – 3757
Departmental numbers	none
Internal user numbers	none
Examples extant	none

These were rebuilt from the large cattle wagons to diagram 1515, of which nearly 400 were built, and were for the conveyance of prize cattle. The major external differences to ordinary cattle wagons of diagram 1515 was the addition of slats instead of open windows and more closely boarded body sides. They were also uprated to run in passenger trains.

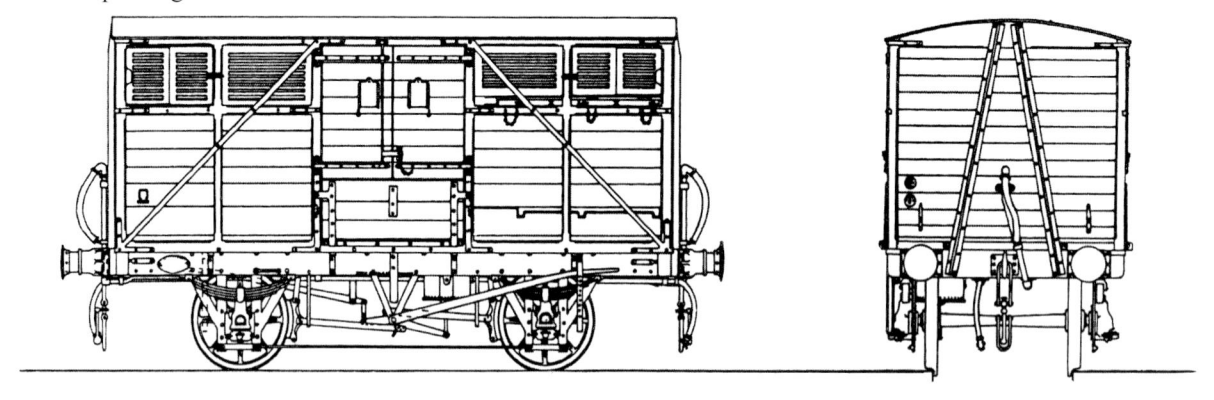

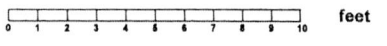

SECR/SR special cattle van (diagram 1051). (Mike King)

SECR/SR special cattle van number 3770. (John Smith)

CATTLE WAGONS AND SPECIAL CATTLE VANS

LBSCR large cattle wagon

Built by or for	LBSCR
SR diagram number	1528 (some rebuilt to 1457)
Description	10-ton large cattle wagon
Quantity built	20
Date	1922
Quantity at Nationalisation	3 (diagram 1457)
Underframe material	timber
Wheelbase	11' 2"
Body length	18' 4"
Overall length	21' 4"
Body width	8' 0"
Height above rails	11' 11½"
SR running numbers	53282 – 53301, IOW 53371 – 53376, 53374 – 53376 rebuilt and renumbered 46924 – 46926
Departmental number	1066s ex 46924
Internal user numbers	none
Example extant	46924
Location	WightR

These were virtually the same as cattle wagons to diagram 1527, of which 400 were built. Three were converted to covered goods wagons to diagram 1457 in 1935 for use on the Isle of Wight. The main differences to their appearance was the replacement of the normal type of cattle wagon doors with a pair of goods van style hinged doors. End ventilators were added.

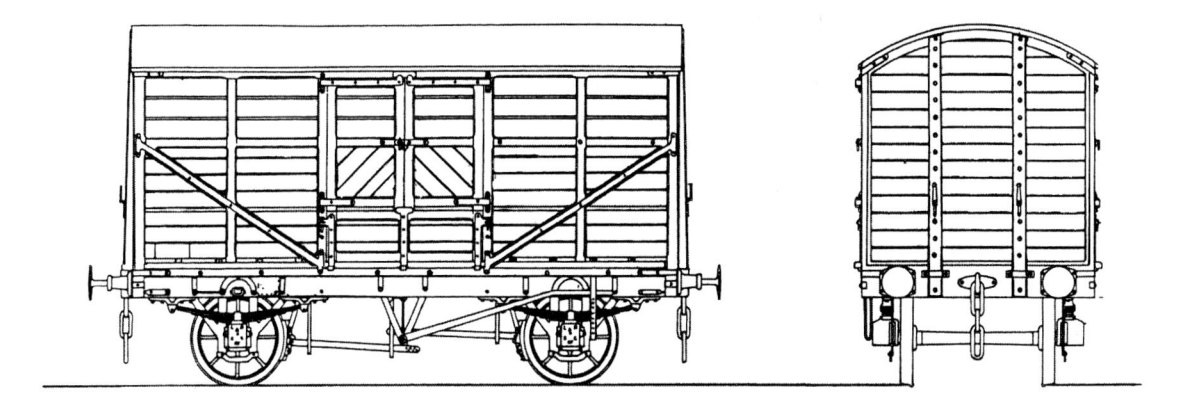

LBSCR large cattle wagon (diagram 1527). (Gerry Bixley)

LBSCR large cattle wagons numbers S53371 and 53372 photographed post-1948 on the Isle of Wight. (John Smith)

Above and below: LBSCR large cattle wagon number 46924 (ex 53374) photographed at Sandown on 14th August 1966. (Terry Gough)

CATTLE WAGONS AND SPECIAL CATTLE VANS

SR/BR special cattle van

Built by or for	SR/BR
SR diagram number	3141
Description	8/12-ton special cattle van (SR CATOX; BR SCV)
Quantity built	60
Dates	1930 and 1952
Quantity at Nationalisation	50 (that is, all)
Underframe material	steel
Wheelbase	17' 6"
Body length	26' 0"
Overall length	29' 5"
Body width	8' 0"
Height above rails	11' 9"
SR running numbers	3679 – 3738
Departmental numbers	DS70191 ex 3703, DS70190 ex 3716
Internal user numbers	none
Examples extant	3716 3733
Location	Bo'nessR ShildonM

These vans were passenger rated but included here for convenience. Wheel diameter is 3'1½". The centre compartment was for the groom. The windows are opposite one another, that is to the left of the door on one side and right of the door on the other side (as can be seen in the photographs).

Above: SR/BR special cattle van number S3737S photographed at Micheldever in August 1968. (Terry Gough)

Right: End detail of van pictured above. (Terry Gough)

33

A PICTORIAL GUIDE TO SOUTHERN WAGONS AND VANS

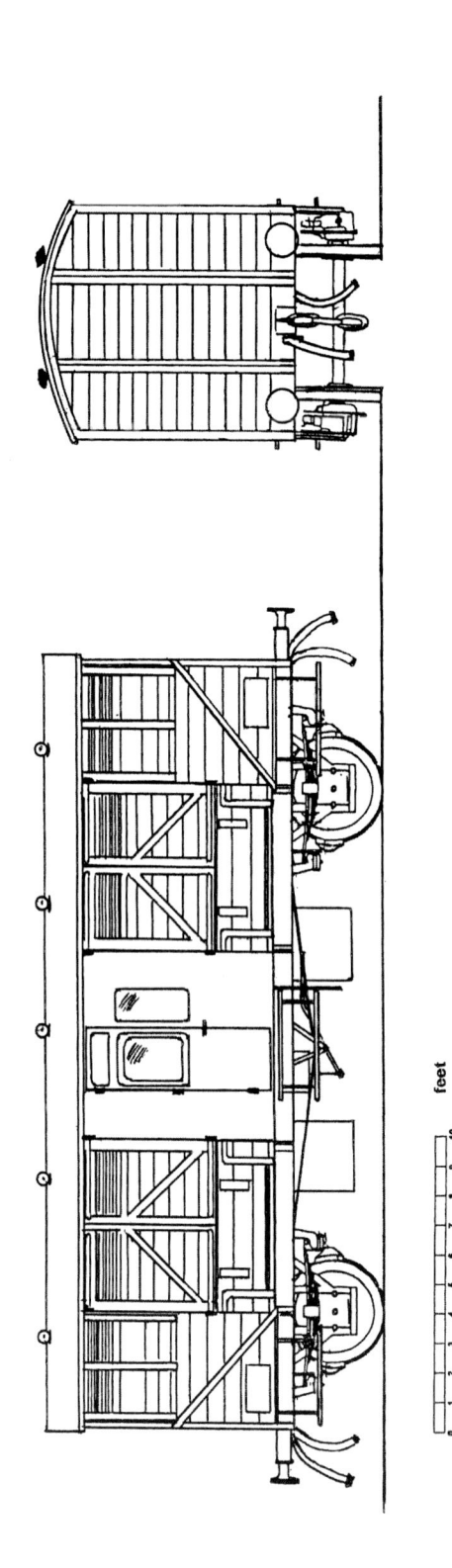

Above: SR/BR special cattle van (diagram 3141). (Terry Gough)

Below: Detail from both sides of SR/BR special cattle van no S37375, photographed at Micheldever on 15th October 1971. (Terry Gough)

CATTLE WAGONS AND SPECIAL CATTLE VANS

SR/BR special cattle van number S3734S photographed at Barry in August 1968. (Terry Gough)

SR/BR large cattle wagon

Built by or for	SR	SR/BR
SR diagram number	1529	1530, 1/351
Description	10-ton large cattle wagon	10/12-ton large cattle wagon
Approximate quantity built	300	400
Dates	1930 – 1939	1947 – 1949
Quantity at Nationalisation	all	251 (that is, all)
Underframe material	steel	steel
Wheelbase	10' 6"	10' 6"
Body length	19' 0"	19' 0"
Overall length	22' 5"	22' 5"
Body width	7' 10"	7' 10"
Height above rails	11' 4"	11' 3"
SR running numbers (examples)	53629 – 53844	52268 – 52578, B891250 – 891399
Departmental numbers	none	several
Internal user numbers	none	none
Example extant	none known	B891364
Location		MangappsR

Vehicles to diagram 1530 had plywood body ends. All were vacuum piped or brake fitted. The surviving vehicle had been used as a tunnel inspection wagon for which it was cut down. It has been restored to virtually original condition.

SR/BR large cattle wagon number S53732 photographed post-1948. (John Smith)

A PICTORIAL GUIDE TO SOUTHERN WAGONS AND VANS

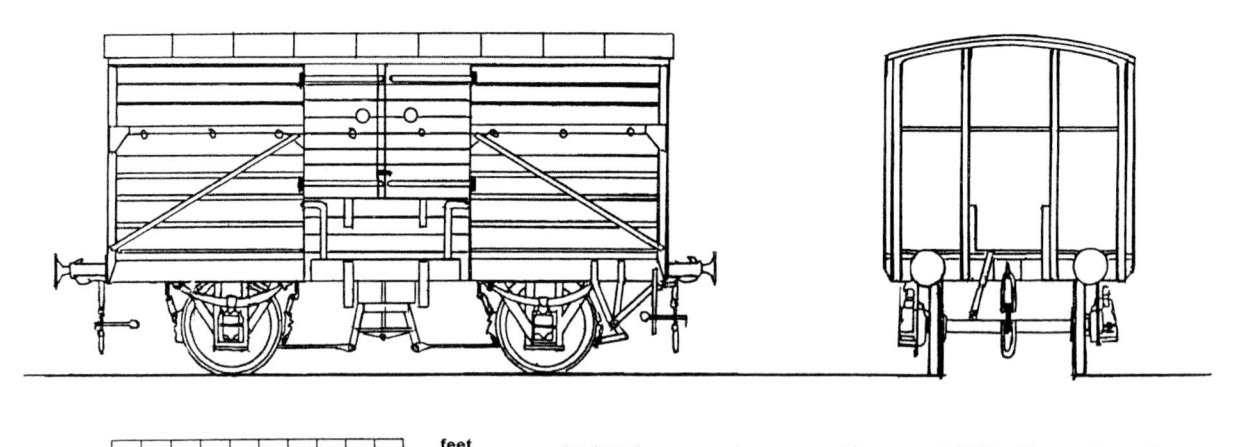

SR/BR large cattle wagon (diagram 1530). (Terry Gough)

Above and below: SR/BR large cattle wagon number B891364 photographed at Burnham on Crouch on 23rd November 2005. (Terry Gough)

Gunpowder Vans

LSWR gunpowder van

Built by or for	LSWR
SR diagram number	1701
Description	7-ton gunpowder van
Quantity built	12
Dates	1904, 1912
Quantity at Nationalisation	all
Underframe material	steel
Wheelbase	9' 0"
Body length	16' 0"
Overall length	19' 0"
Body width	7' 5"
Height above rails	10' 7"
SR running numbers	61201 – 61212
Departmental numbers	KDS61209
Internal user numbers	080407
Examples extant	LSWR 1904 (ex 61209) GWR 105493 GWR 105742
Location	YeovilC WSomR EmbsayR

Most of these vehicles were built by contractors and were virtually identical to those built for the GWR.

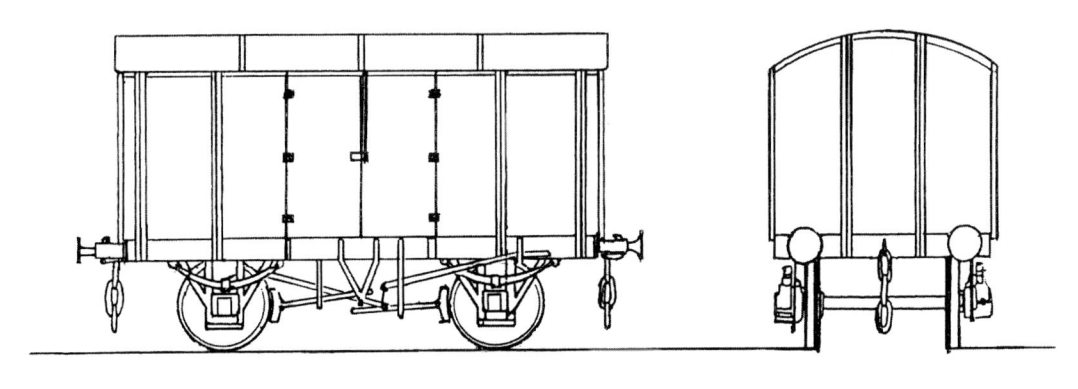

LSWR gunpowder van (diagram 1701). (Terry Gough)

GWR gunpowder van number W105493 photographed at Barry on 25th August 1981. (Terry Gough)

Above and right: LSWR gunpowder van, number 1904, photographed at Yeovil Junction on 6th *April 2007. (Terry Gough)*

Model of LSWR gunpowder van number 61204 (diagram 1701). (Terry Gough)

Goods Brake Vans

Class Q1 No 33010 on a Feltham to Woking freight train near Addlestone on 31st July 1963. The first vehicle is an SR 25-ton brake van to diagram 1579. (Terry Gough)

It is surprising to find so many designs of goods brake vans, despite the fact that all had the same purpose. The SR inherited nine types from the LSWR and a similar number from the LBSCR. The SR produced its own standard 4-wheeled brake van, which with minor variations was allocated six different diagram numbers. The SR also built the ultimate in brake vans, the express bogie van.

LSWR goods brake van

Built by or for	LSWR
SR diagram number	1541
Description	10-, 11- and 15-ton goods brake van
Approximate quantity built	450
Dates	1887 – 1905
Quantity at Nationalisation	unknown
Underframe material	timber
Wheelbase	10' 6"
Body length	18' 0"
Overall length	21' 0"
Body width	7' 9½"
Height above rails	11' 2"
SR running numbers (examples)	54501 – 54734, IOW 56044 – 56055
Departmental number (example)	DS54538
Internal user numbers	none known
Examples extant	54885 56046 56055
Location	WSomR WightR YorkM

Brake vans that had side doors through which parcels could be loaded were sometimes referred to as road vans.

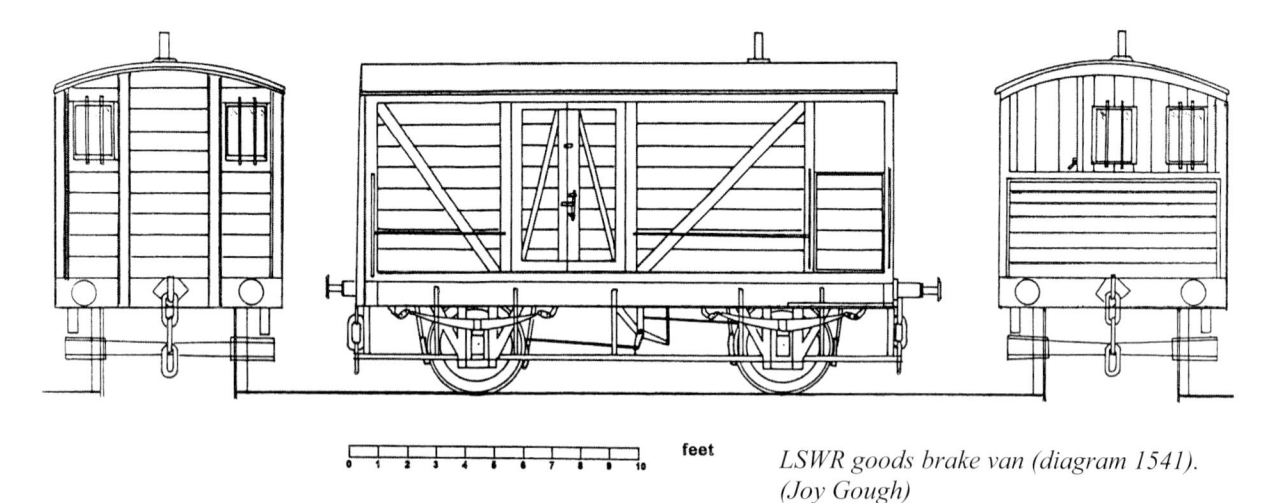

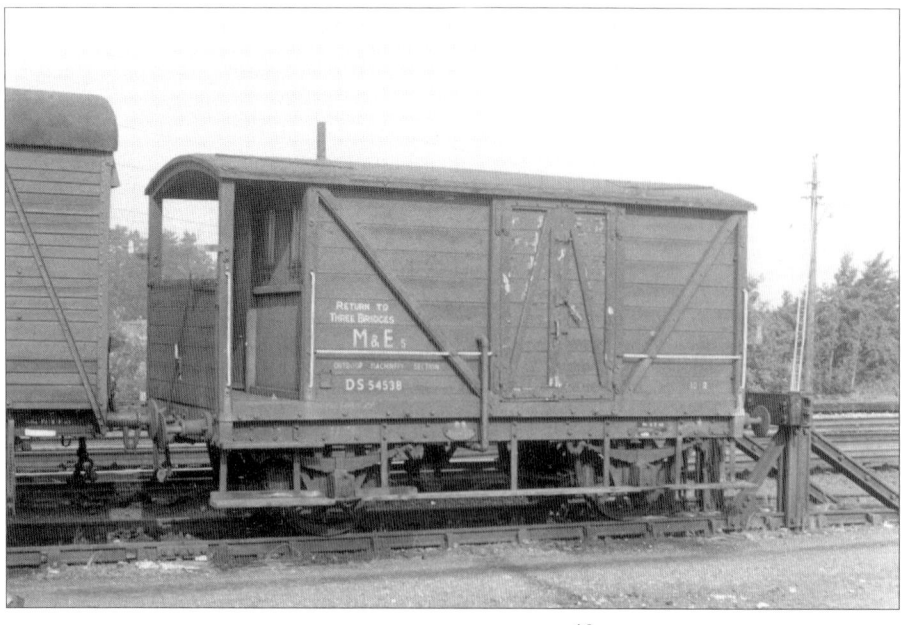

LSWR goods brake van (diagram 1541). (Joy Gough)

LSWR goods brake van number DS54538 photographed at Three Bridges in June 1967. (Terry Gough)

GOODS BRAKE VANS

Above: LSWR goods brake van number S56055 photographed at Medina Wharf on 12th August 1965. (Terry Gough)

Right: LSWR goods brake van number S56053 photographed at Newport in December 1966. (Terry Gough)

Model of LSWR goods brake van number 54538 (diagram 1541). (Terry Gough)

A PICTORIAL GUIDE TO SOUTHERN WAGONS AND VANS

LSWR/SR goods brake van

Built by or for	LSWR/SR
SR diagram number	none, rebuilt from 1541
Description	10-ton goods brake van
Quantity built	4
Date	1933
Quantity at Nationalisation	all
Underframe material	timber
Wheelbase	10' 6"
Body length	18' 0"
Overall length	21' 0"
Body width	7' 9½"
Height above rails	11' 2"
SR running numbers	IOW 56044, 56047 – 56049
Departmental numbers	none
Internal user numbers	none
Examples extant	none

These are rebuilds of vans to diagram 1541 (page 40) for the Isle of Wight, with an additional and much larger veranda.

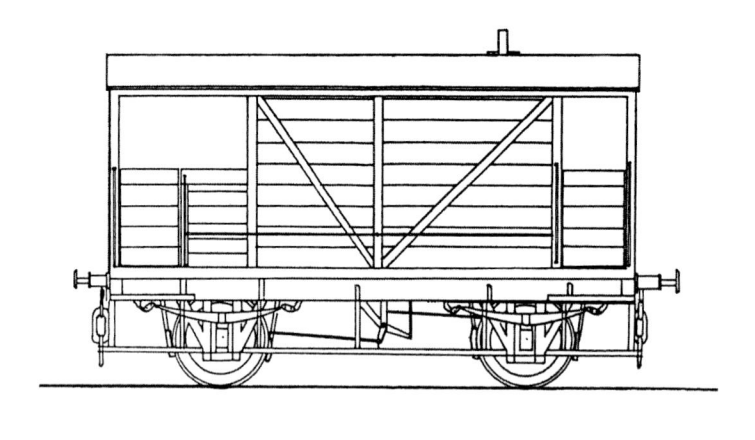

LSWR/SR goods brake van (rebuilt from diagram 1541). (Terry Gough)

LSWR/SR goods brake van number S56048 photographed at Newport on 20th September 1965. (Terry Gough)

GOODS BRAKE VANS

LSWR goods brake van

Built by or for	LSWR
SR diagram number	1542
Description	18-ton goods brake van
Quantity built	4
Date	1906
Underframe material	timber
Wheelbase	14' 0"
Body length	24' 0"
Overall length	27 0"
Body width	7' 9", 8'9" over duckets
Height above rails	11' 2"
SR running numbers	54945 – 54948, to IOW 56058 ex 54948
Departmental numbers	none
Internal user numbers	none
Examples extant	none

These were built as 6-wheeled vans, but were soon converted to 4-wheelers.

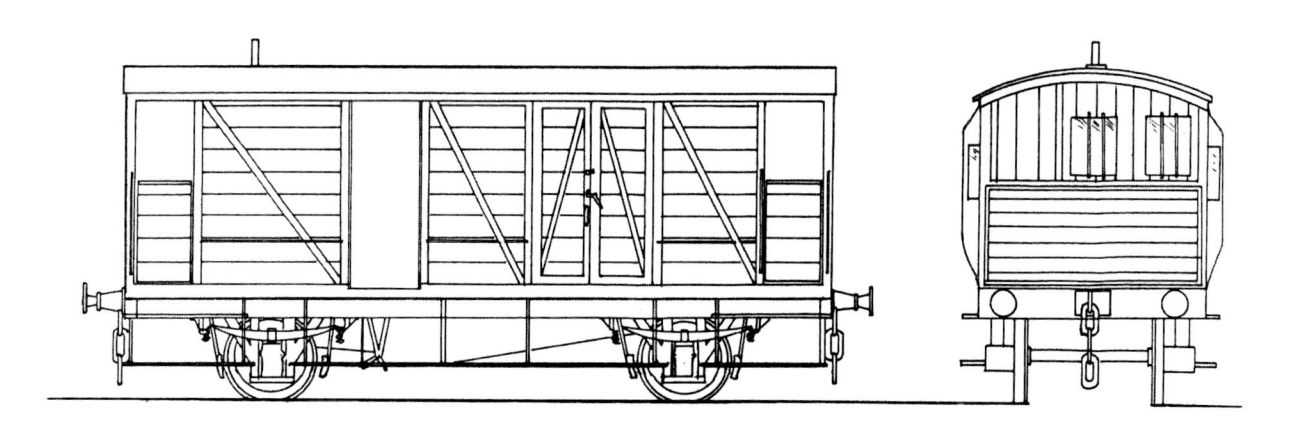

LSWR goods brake van (diagram 1542). (Terry Gough)

Model of LSWR goods brake van number 56058 (diagram 1542). (Terry Gough)

A PICTORIAL GUIDE TO SOUTHERN WAGONS AND VANS

Above and right: LSWR goods brake van number S56058 photographed at Newport on 12th August 1965. (Terry Gough)

44

GOODS BRAKE VANS

LSWR goods brake van

Built by or for	LSWR
SR diagram number	1543
Description	20/25-ton goods brake van
Quantity built	75
Date	1915 – 1921
Quantity at Nationalisation	majority
Underframe material	steel
Wheelbase	13' 0"
Body length	20' 0"
Overall length	23' 0"
Body width	7' 9½", 8' 9" over duckets
Height above rails	11' 8"
SR running numbers (examples)	55019 – 55074
Departmental numbers	none known
Internal user number	080673
Examples extant	none known

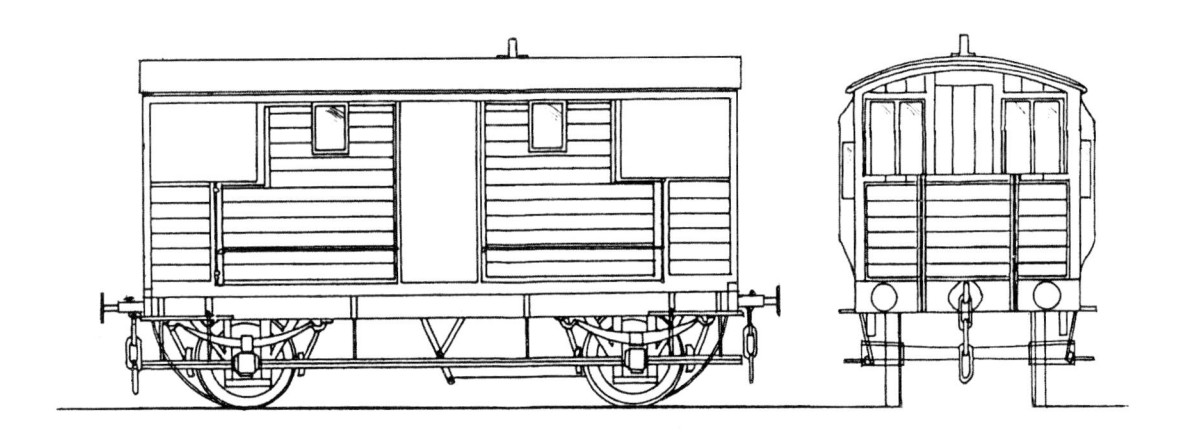

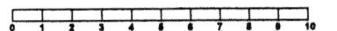

LSWR goods brake van (diagram 1543). (Terry Gough)

LSWR goods brake van number S55037 photographed at Guildford on 26th June 1960. (David Wigley)

A PICTORIAL GUIDE TO SOUTHERN WAGONS AND VANS

SECR 6-wheeled goods brake van

Built by or for	SECR
SR diagram number	1558
Description	20-ton 6-wheeled goods brake van
Quantity built	90
Date	1898 – 1914
Quantity at Nationalisation	86
Underframe material	steel (12" solebar)
Wheelbase	5' 0" + 5' 0"
Body length	18' 1"
Overall length	21' 0"
Body width	7' 6"
Height above rails	10' 11½"
SR running numbers	55366 – 55455
Departmental numbers (examples)	DS55380, DS55419
Internal user number	008xxxx ex 55418
Examples extant	55371
Location	KESR

The photograph shows one of the first batch of vans, which originally had one veranda open. Note that the two ends are not the same on these vans. From 1910 vans were built with both verandas enclosed.

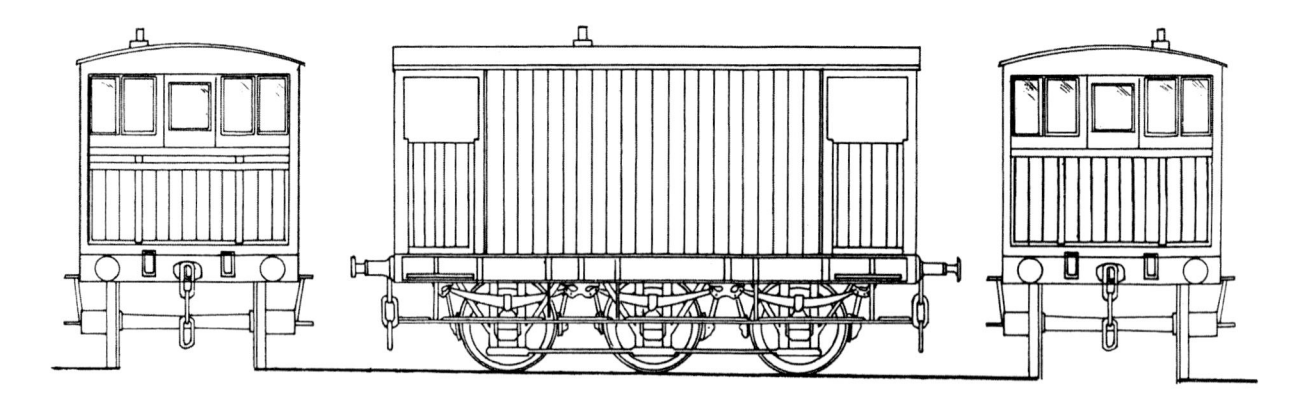

SECR 6-wheeled goods brake van (diagram 1558). (Terry Gough)

Model of SECR 6-wheeled goods brake van number 55371 (diagram 1558). (Terry Gough)

46

GOODS BRAKE VANS

SECR 6-wheeled goods brake van, formerly numbered 55371, photographed at Rolvenden in May 1967. (Terry Gough)

Left: Centre wheels.

Bottom left: Outer wheels.

Below: End view.

SECR/SR goods brake van

Built by or for	SECR	SR
SR diagram number	1559	1560
Description	25-ton goods brake van	
Quantity built	20	40
Date	1918 and 1921	1923 – 1927
Quantity at Nationalisation	all	all
Underframe material	steel (12" solebar)	steel (15" solebar)
Wheelbase	16' 0"	16' 0"
Body length	24' 0"	24' 0"
Overall length	27' 0"	27' 0"
Body width	7' 10"	7' 10"
Height above rails	12' 0"	12' 0"
SR running numbers (examples)	55456 – 55475	55476 – 55515
Departmental numbers (examples)	DS55467, DS55472	DS55488, DS55496
Internal user numbers	none known	none known
Examples extant		55477, 55490 55513
Location		BluebellR MangappsR

Ten of the vans to diagram 1560 were rebuilt to diagram 1761 (page 83) for engineers' use and renumbered.

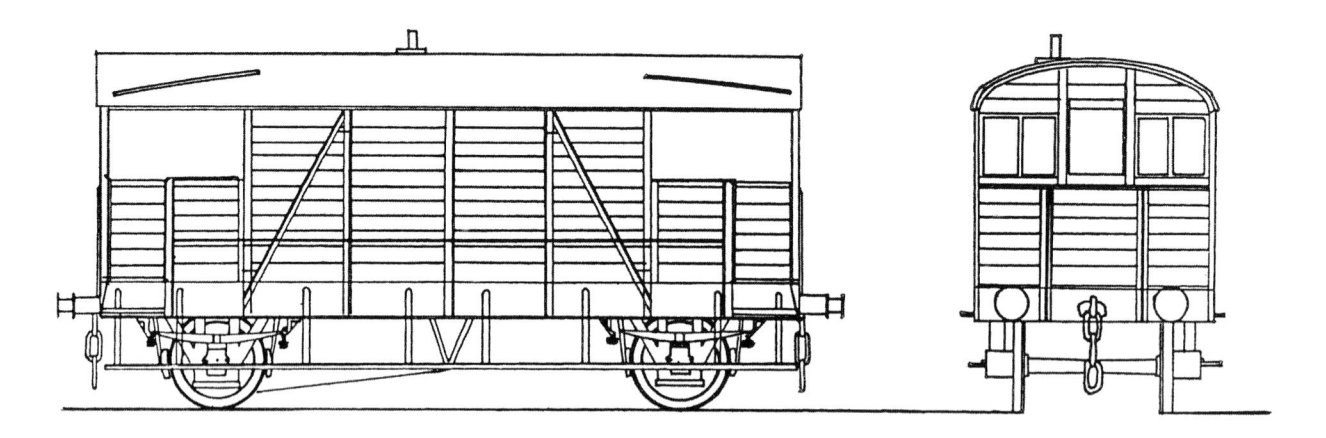

SR goods brake van (diagram 1560). (Terry Gough)

Left: SECR/SR goods brake van number DS55496 photographed at Woking in June 1968. (Terry Gough)

Opposite page, bottom: Model of SECR/SR goods brake van number 55496 (diagram 1560). (Terry Gough)

GOODS BRAKE VANS

Above: SECR/SR goods brake van number DS55472 photographed at Wimbledon in November 1965.

Right: SECR/SR goods brake van number DS55476 photographed at Nine Elms in January 1969.

Below: Detail from SECR/SR goods brake van number DS55505 photographed at Nine Elms in January 1969. (All Terry Gough)

49

A PICTORIAL GUIDE TO SOUTHERN WAGONS AND VANS

LBSCR/SR goods brake van

Built by or for	LBSCR/SR
SR diagram number	1576
Description	20-ton goods brake van
Quantity built	31
Date	1922/23
Quantity at Nationalisation	29
Underframe material	steel
Wheelbase	16' 0"
Body length	24' 0"
Overall length	27' 0"
Body width	8' 0"
Height above rails	11' 9"
SR running numbers	55897 – 55927
Departmental number (example)	DS55907
Internal user numbers	none known
Examples extant	none

About half were rebuilt to diagram 1760 (page 84) for engineers' use and renumbered.

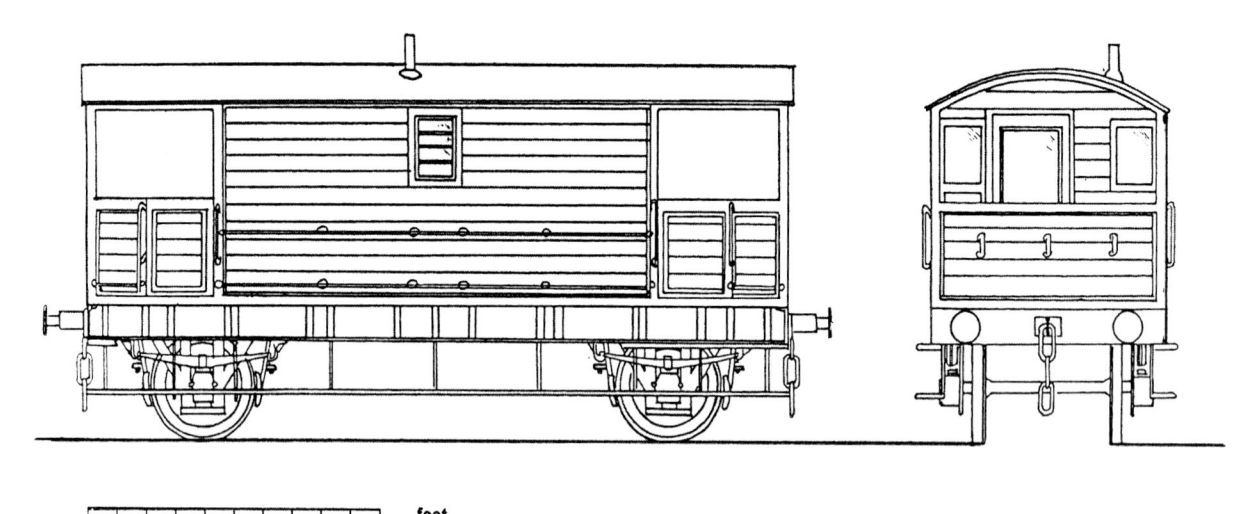

LBSCR/SR goods brake van (diagram 1576). (Joy Gough)

Model of LBSCR/SR goods brake van number 55907 (diagram 1576). (Terry Gough)

GOODS BRAKE VANS

Above: LBSCR/SR goods brake van number DS55907 photographed at Three Bridges in May 1967.

Right: Veranda detail from the same van.

Below: End detail from the same van.
(All Terry Gough)

SR goods brake van

Built by or for	SR
SR diagram number	1578
Description	25-ton goods brake van
Quantity built	80
Date	1928/29
Quantity at Nationalisation	probably all
Underframe material	steel
Wheelbase	16' 0"
Body length	13' 11"
Length over headstocks	24' 0"
Overall length	27' 0"
Body width	6' 11", 8' 4" over duckets
Height above rails	11' 5"
SR running numbers (examples)	55943 – 55992, 55552/4/6/8
Departmental numbers (examples)	DS55556, DS55961
Internal user numbers	none known
Example extant	55550
Location	NeneR

This is the first version of what became the standard SR brake van. These vans have the same underframes as vehicles to diagram 1560. Bodies are left handed with respect to duckets.

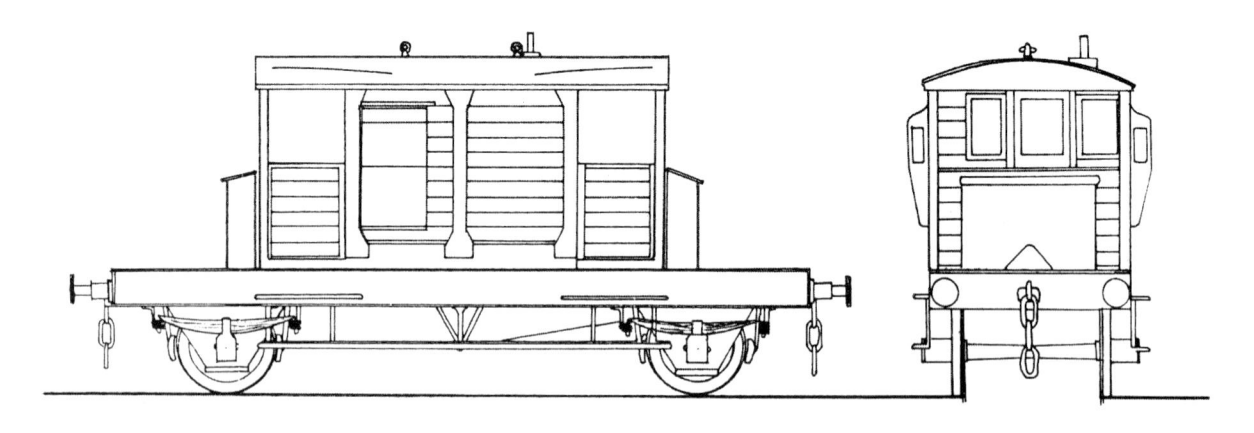

SR goods brake van (diagram 1578). (Terry Gough)

SR goods brake van number DS55556 photographed at Woking in October 1968. (Terry Gough)

GOODS BRAKE VANS

SR goods brake vans

Built by or for	SR/MoS	SR
SR diagram number	1579	1582
Description	25-ton goods brake vans	
Approximate quantity built	500	100
Date	1929 – 1943	1947/48
Quantity at Nationalisation	all	all
Underframe material	steel	steel
Wheelbase	16' 0"	16' 0"
Body length	13' 11"	13' 11"
Length over headstocks	24' 0"	24' 0"
Overall length	27' 0"	27' 0"
Body width	6' 11", 8' 4" over duckets	6' 11", 8' 4" over duckets
Height above rails	11' 5"	11' 5"
SR running numbers (examples)	55551/3/5/7	55121 – 55170
Equal width planking	55566 – 55585	
Alternate wide/narrow planking	56327 – 56351	
Departmental numbers	DS55574, DS55585, KDS56153	
Internal user numbers	none known	
Examples extant and location	AD49004 (PlymR), AD49012 (SwanageR), AD49014 (BucksR), AD49015 (YeovilC), AD49027(EKR), 55126(GlosR), 56010 (GCR), KDS56153 (IcknieldR), 56451 (PlymR)	

Bodies are right handed with respect to duckets. Some had bodies constructed of equal width planking, whereas on others the planking was alternately wide and narrow pairs. Some vans had a single window in the body end and others had two windows. They were built with a large sandbox outside each veranda, but these were later removed. Vans to diagram 1582 had different sanding and brake gear.

The vehicles built for the Ministry of Supply had automatic vacuum and Westinghouse brake equipment. The major visual difference to the vans built for the SR was two large vacuum cylinders on the platform at one end.

SR goods brake van number S56351 photographed at Woking in July 1965. (Terry Gough)

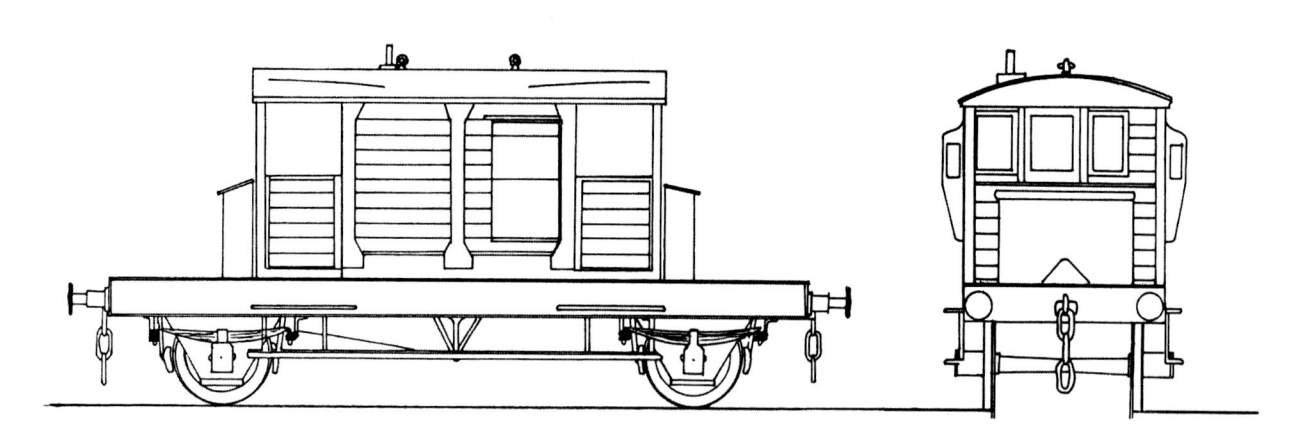

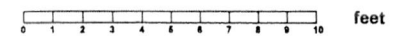

A PICTORIAL GUIDE TO SOUTHERN WAGONS AND VANS

SR goods brake van (diagram 1579). (Terry Gough)

Above: *SR goods brake van number DS55574 photographed at Woking on 31st August 1968. (Terry Gough)*

Right: *Detail from van pictured above. (Terry Gough)*

GOODS BRAKE VANS

Above: SR goods brake van number S55146 photographed at Barry in August 1968. (Terry Gough)

Right: Detail from van pictured above. (Terry Gough)

Below: Model of SR goods brake van number 56110 (diagram 1579). (Terry Gough)

55

A PICTORIAL GUIDE TO SOUTHERN WAGONS AND VANS

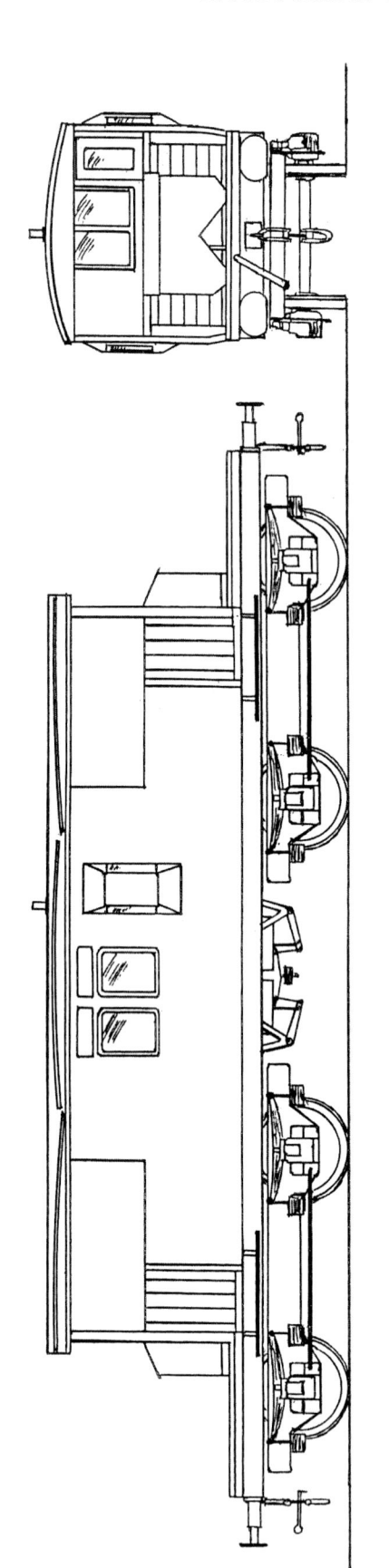

LBSCR/SR bogie goods brake van (diagram 1580). (Terry Gough)

LBSCR/SR bogie goods brake van number DS56281 photographed at an unknown location, post-1948. (John Smith)

LBSCR/SR bogie goods brake van number 56264 photographed at an unknown location, pre-1948. (John Smith)

GOODS BRAKE VANS

LBSCR/SR bogie goods brake van

Built by or for	LBSCR/SR
SR diagram number	1580
Description	27-ton bogie goods brake van
Quantity built	21
Date	1933
Quantity at Nationalisation	20
Underframe material	steel
Bogie centres	21' 5"
Wheelbase	8' 9"
Body length	26' 11"
Length over headstocks	38' 4"
Overall length	42' 0"
Body width	8' 0", 8' 11" over duckets
Height above rails	11' 5"
SR running numbers	56261 – 56281
Departmental number (example)	DS56281
Internal user numbers	none known
Examples extant	none

These vehicles were constructed from ex LBSCR motor luggage vans. Both sides are shown in the photographs opposite, from which it can be seen that they are not identical.

SR goods brake van

Built by or for	SR
SR diagram number	1581
Description	15-ton goods brake van
Quantity built	50
Date	1934
Quantity at Nationalisation	48
Underframe material	steel (10" solebar)
Wheelbase	16' 0"
Body length	13' 11"
Length over headstocks	24' 0"
Overall length	27' 0"
Body width	6' 11", 8' 4" over duckets
Height above rails	11' 2"
SR running numbers	55675 – 55724
Departmental numbers (examples)	DS455 (ex 55719), many others
Internal user numbers	none known
Examples extant	55710 55719? 55724
Location	WightR MangappsR WightR

The bodies were identical to diagram 1579 (see page 54), but height was less because these vehicles had shallower solebars. Most retained their sandboxes.

Two vans were converted for use in weed killing trains and had a locker for petrol cans (see bottom photograph on page 58). They were given diagram 1891.

A PICTORIAL GUIDE TO SOUTHERN WAGONS AND VANS

Above: SR goods brake van number 55675 photographed at Alton in June 1968. (Terry Gough)

Right: Roof detail of SR goods brake van number S55698 photographed at Horsham in May 1968. (Terry Gough)

Below: SR goods brake van number DS455 photographed at Horsham in May 1968. (Terry Gough)

GOODS BRAKE VANS

SR bogie goods brake van

Built by or for	SR
SR diagram number	1550
Description	25-ton bogie goods brake van
Quantity built	25
Date	1936
Quantity at Nationalisation	all
Underframe material	steel
Bogie centres	21' 0"
Bogie wheelbase	8' 0"
Body length	24' 5"
Length over headstocks	36' 6"
Overall length	39' 9"
Body width	7' 6" over roof, 8' 4" over duckets
Height above rails	11' 4"
SR running numbers	56282 – 56306
Departmental numbers	several
Examples extant and location	56287 (WorthR), 56290 (BluebellR), 56291 (SevernR), 56297 (YorkM), 56302 (SwanageR), ADS56303 (National Network), KDS56305 (GlosR)

Some vans had all timber body sides, whereas others had varying amounts of steel sheeting as shown on the photographs on this page and on page 60. They were all fitted with standard SR bogies (see illustration under diagram 3191 on page 147).

SR bogie goods brake van number DS56291 photographed at Surbiton in October 1971. (Terry Gough)

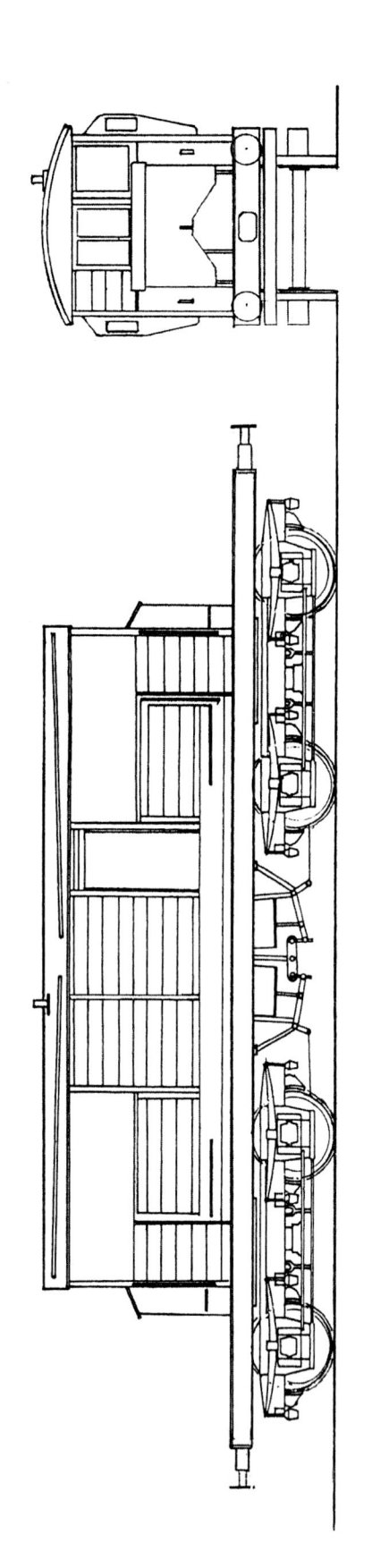

A PICTORIAL GUIDE TO SOUTHERN WAGONS AND VANS

SR bogie goods brake van (diagram 1550). (Terry Gough)

Veranda detail from the same van. (Terry Gough)

SR bogie goods brake van number S56302 photographed at Surbiton in August 1968. (Terry Gough)

GOODS BRAKE VANS

SR bogie goods brake van number 56287 photographed at Ingrow West on 7th June 2006.
(Terry Gough)

Detail from SR bogie goods brake van number S56294 photographed at Surbiton in January 1969.
(Terry Gough)

Model of SR bogie goods brake van number 56288 (diagram 1550).
(Terry Gough)

Bolster Wagons

40-ton bogie bolster wagon number DS57849 photographed at Woking on 30th August 1969. (Terry Gough)

LSWR/SR bogie bolster wagon

Built by or for	LSWR/SR
SR diagram number	1597
Description	40-ton bogie bolster wagon
Quantity built	100
Date	1916 – 1926
Quantity at Nationalisation	all
Underframe material	steel
Bogie centres	34' 6"
Wheelbase	5' 6"
Length over headstocks	47' 6"
Overall length	50' 6"
Body width	8' 8½", stanchions are on the flatbed
SR running numbers	57783 – 57882
Departmental numbers	several including DS57840, DS57849
Internal user numbers (examples)	083561 ex 57837, 083562 ex ADS57838, 083563 ex 57842
Example extant	57849
Location	HantsR

BOLSTER WAGONS

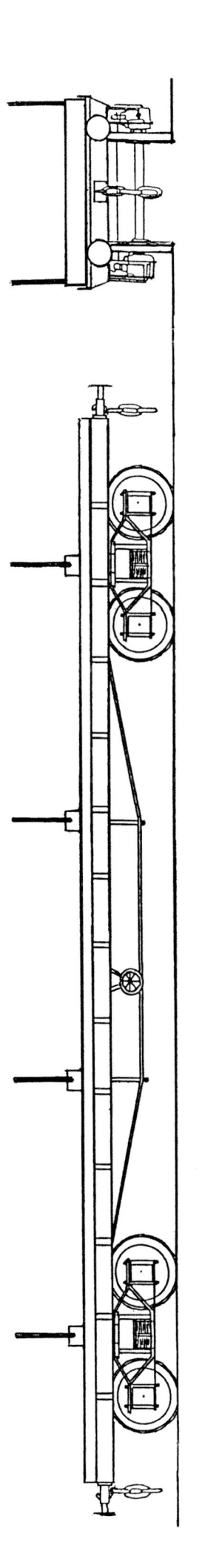

LSWR/SR bogie bolster wagon (diagram 1597). (Terry Gough)

Detail from LSWR/SR bogie bolster wagon number DS57849 photographed at Woking on 30th August 1969. (Terry Gough)

LBSCR single bolster wagon

Built by or for	LBSCR
SR diagram number	1616, 1619
Description	6-ton single bolster wagon (1616), many upgraded to 10-ton (1619)
Approximate quantity built	200
Date	1880 – 1911
Quantity at Nationalisation	35
Underframe material	timber
Wheelbase	7' 0"
Length over headstocks	12' 0"
Overall length	15' 0"
Width	7' 10"
SR running numbers	58277 – 58468, to IOW 59037 – 59052 except 59046
Departmental numbers (examples)	ADS59043, ADS59045
Internal user numbers	None
Examples extant	59038/45/49/50
Location	WightR

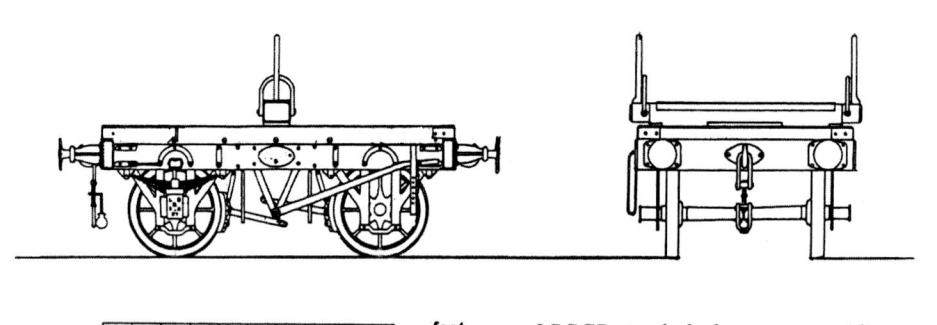

LBSCR single bolster wagon (diagram 1616). (Gerry Bixley)

LBSCR single bolster wagon number DS59039 photographed at Newport on 12th August 1965. (Terry Gough)

BOLSTER WAGONS

LBSCR single bolster wagons numbers DS59042, DS59051, DS59049 and DS59038 photographed at Newport on 12th August 1965. (Terry Gough)

SR bogie bolster wagons

Built by or for	SR	SR
SR diagram number	1598	1599
Description	40-ton bogie bolster wagons (rail wagons)	
Quantity built	105	69
Date	1937 – 1945	1946 – 1948
Quantity at Nationalisation	majority	all
Underframe material	steel	steel
Bogie centres	49' 6"	49' 6"
Bogie type	LSWR	SR cast
Wheelbase	5' 6"	5' 6"
Length over headstocks	64' 0"	64' 0"
Overall length	67' 1"	67' 1"
Width over stanchions	8' 4"	8' 4"
SR running numbers	57883 – 57987	57988 – 58039, 64738 – 64754
Departmental numbers (examples)	DS64622 – 64646	DS64753
Internal user numbers	083312 ex DS64634, 083310 ex DS64641	083308 ex 58021, 083306 ex 64753
Examples extant		57989 64752
Location		HantsR MoorsR

Photographs of the bogies are under diagram 1597 for LSWR (page 63) and 1775 (page 91) for SR.
Floors are steel plate overlaid with timber.
Number 58038 is illustrated on page 81.

65

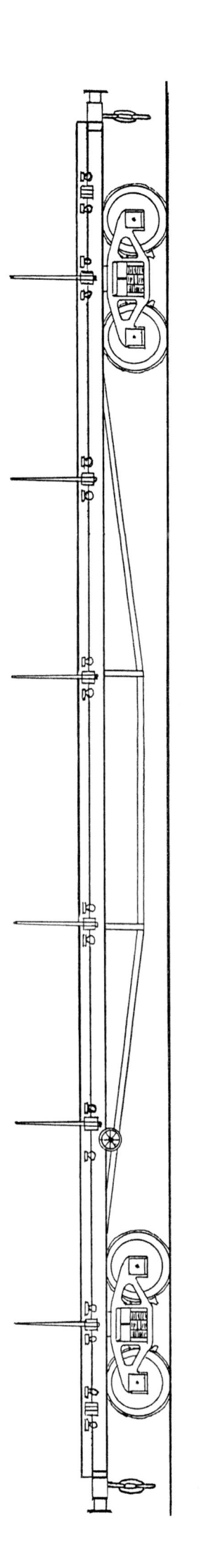

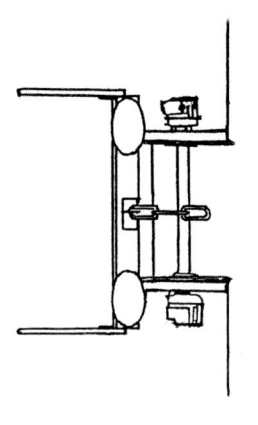

Above: SR bogie bolster wagon (diagram 1599). (Terry Gough)

Left: SR bogie bolster wagon number S57923 photographed at New Cross Gate on 21st September 1971. (Terry Gough)

66

TRUCKS

Trucks (Vehicle, Machinery and Container)

One of several long freight trains arriving at Woking on 23rd December 1961. The third container truck from the front is SR, the others being of BR origin. Further down the train, under the signal gantry, is a standard SR covered van. The engine is ex LSWR Class S15 No 30496, to the right of which is Class U No 31628 on another freight train. (Terry Gough)

Containers from the adjacent abattoir being attached to the rear of the 3.13 pm Padstow to Waterloo train at Halwill Junction on 5th July 1961 by Class N No 31833. Not surprisingly all the containers and the trucks are BR, as by this time almost all the SR stock had been withdrawn. The single coach (Bulleid brake composite No 6727) on the left will form the 6.40 pm to Torrington behind Class 2MT No 41298. (Terry Gough)

A PICTORIAL GUIDE TO SOUTHERN WAGONS AND VANS

LSWR road vehicle truck

Built by or for	LSWR
SR diagram number	1641
Description	10-ton road vehicle truck
Quantity built	59
Date	1888 – 1889
Quantity at Nationalisation	3
Underframe material	timber
Wheelbase	9' 0"
Length over headstocks	16' 0"
Overall length	19' 0"
Width	8' 0"
Height above rails	4' 11½"
SR running numbers	60001 – 60058, 60267, some to IOW and renumbered 60561 – 60564
Departmental number	DS60562 ex 60020
Internal user numbers	none known
Example extant	DS60562
Location	YeovilC

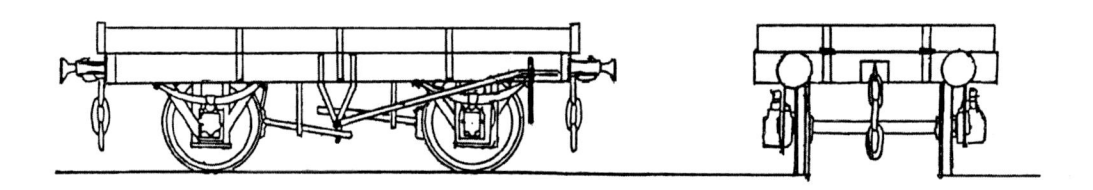

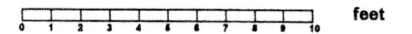

LSWR road vehicle truck (diagram 1641). (Terry Gough)

LSWR road vehicle truck number DS60562 photographed at Yeovil Junction on 22nd December 2005. (Terry Gough)

TRUCKS

Detail from LSWR road vehicle truck number DS60562 photographed at Yeovil Junction on 22ndDecember 2005. (Terry Gough)

LBSCR/SR road vehicle truck

Built by or for	LBSCR/SR
SR diagram number	1661
Description	10-ton road vehicle truck
Quantity built	123
Date	1892 – 1923
Quantity at Nationalisation	40
Underframe material	timber
Wheelbase	10' 5"
Length over headstocks	16' 6"
Overall length	19' 6"
Width	8' 2"
Height above rails	4' 10"
SR running numbers	60423 – 60545, to IOW 60565 – 60583
Departmental numbers (examples)	DS60579, DS60580
Internal user numbers	none
Example extant	60579 ex 60536
Location	WightR

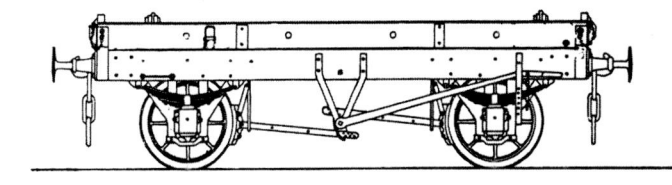

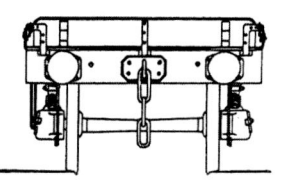

Above: LBSCR/SR road vehicle truck (diagram 1661). (Gerry Bixley)

Right: LBSCR/SR road vehicle truck number DS60579 photographed at Ventnor, probably in the 1960s. (John Smith)

A PICTORIAL GUIDE TO SOUTHERN WAGONS AND VANS

LSWR machinery truck

Built by or for	LSWR
SR diagram number	1676
Description	20-ton machinery truck (Well B)
Quantity built	3
Date	1921
Quantity at Nationalisation	all
Underframe material	steel
Wheelbase	21' 0"
Wheel diameter	2' 9"
Length over headstocks	26' 6"
Overall length	29' 7"
Width	8' 6"
Height above rails	3' 10"
Height of well above rail	2' 4"
SR running numbers	61024, 61027, 61028
Departmental numbers	all
Internal user numbers	none
Example extant	LSWR 11813 (SR 61024)
Location	MoorsR

Above: LSWR machinery truck number DS61024 photographed at Woking on 2nd October 1971. (Terry Gough)

Left: Detail from the truck illustrated above. (Terry Gough)

TRUCKS

LSWR machinery truck (diagram 1676). (Terry Gough)

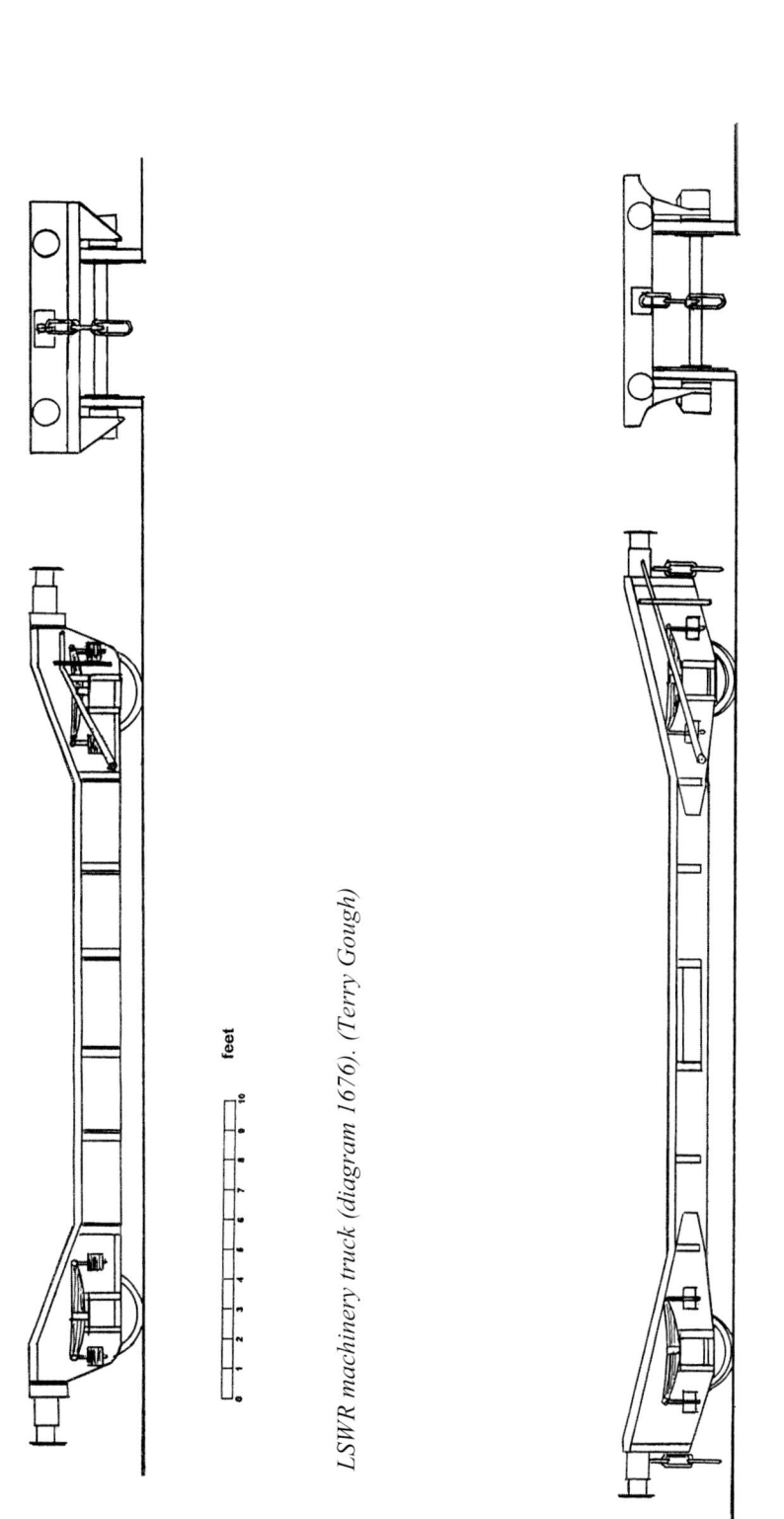

LSWR road vehicle truck (diagram 1681). (Terry Gough)

A PICTORIAL GUIDE TO SOUTHERN WAGONS AND VANS

SECR/SR machinery truck

Built by or for	SECR/SR
SR diagram number	1681
Description	20-ton machinery truck (SR Well B; BR Lowmac SD)
Quantity built	47
Date	1923 – 1942
Quantity at Nationalisation	37
Underframe material	steel
Wheelbase	22' 6"
Wheel diameter	2' 8"
Length over headstocks	29' 6"
Overall length	32' 6"
Width	8' 6"
Height above rails	3' 10½"
Height of well above rail	2' 4"
SR running numbers (examples)	61048 – 61059, 61088 – 61098
Departmental numbers (example)	DS61088, DS61091
Internal user numbers	none known
Examples extant	61048 61056 61095 61155
Location	RotherR WightR SwanageR SwanageR

Right: SECR/SR machinery truck number DS61088 photographed at Woking on 8th March 1969. (Terry Gough)

Below: Details from SECR/SR machinery truck number 61155 photographed at Norden on 13th December 2005. (Terry Gough)

72

TRUCKS

SR well wagon

Built by or for	SR
SR diagram number	1682
Description	20-ton well wagon (Flatrol)
Quantity built	11
Date	1944/45
Quantity at Nationalisation	10
Underframe material	steel
Wheelbase	26' 2"
Wheel diameter	2' 9"
Length over headstocks	32' 2"
Overall length	35' 2"
Width	8' 5"
Height above rails	1' 5"
SR running numbers (examples)	61101 – 61110, 64600
Departmental numbers	DS61107 – 61109
Internal user number	08xxxx ex 64600
Example extant	61107
Location	BluebellR

The floor consisted of removable timbers (for example, sleepers) placed longitudinally between iron cross members. The spacing between successive cross members was adjustable.

Above: SR well wagon number DS61107 photographed at Woking on 2nd October 1971. (Terry Gough)

Left and below: Details from the wagon illustrated above. (Terry Gough)

A PICTORIAL GUIDE TO SOUTHERN WAGONS AND VANS

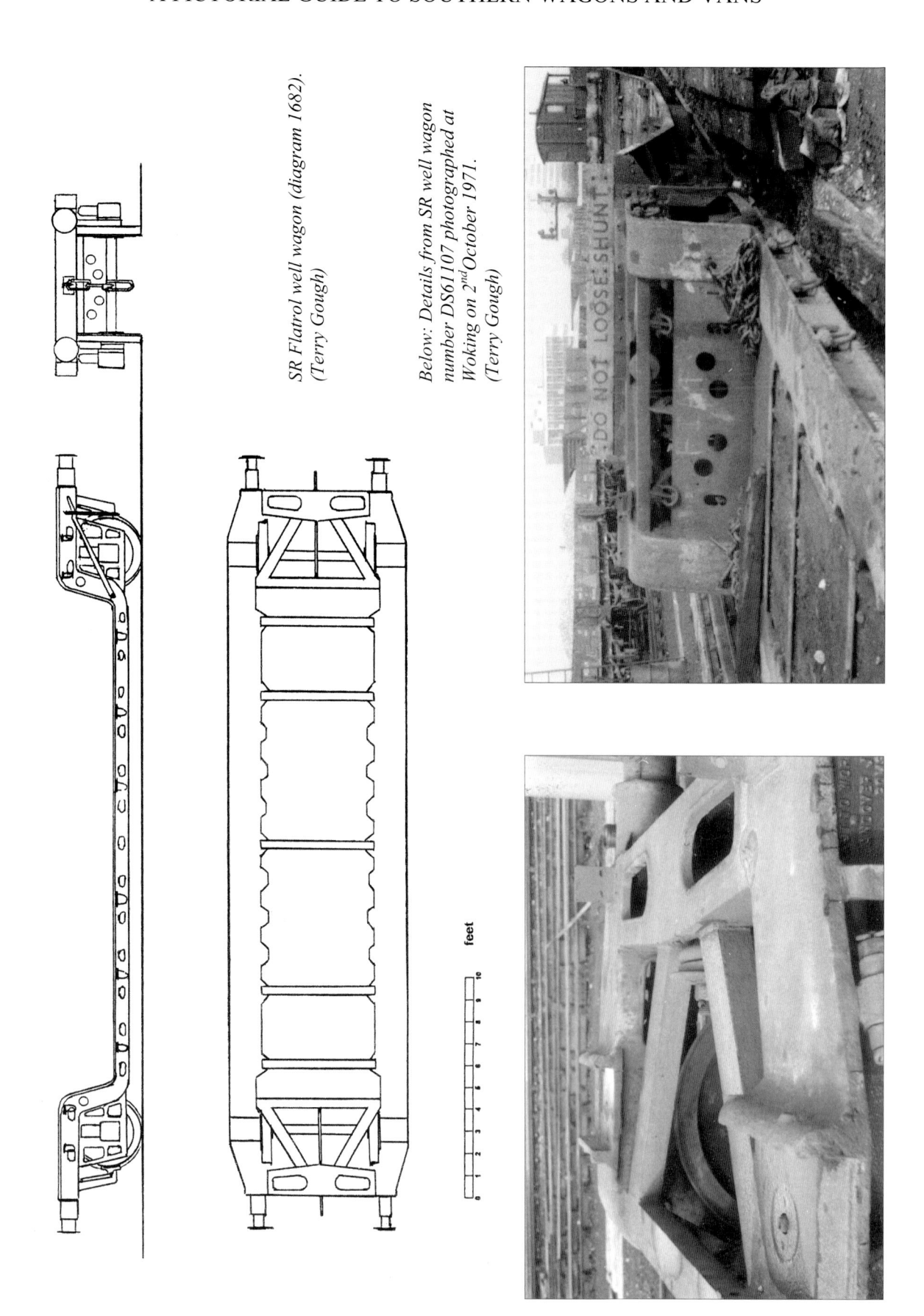

SR Flatrol well wagon (diagram 1682). (Terry Gough)

Below: Details from SR well wagon number DS61107 photographed at Woking on 2nd October 1971. (Terry Gough)

74

TRUCKS

SR container truck (short)

Built by or for	SR	SR
SR diagram number	1382 and 1382A	1399
Description	12/13-ton container truck (short), Conflats A, B and S	
Quantity built	350	755
Date	1931 – 1932	1938 – 1947
Quantity at Nationalisation	349	all
Underframe material	steel	steel
Wheelbase	9' 0"	10' 0"
Length over headstocks	17' 6"	17' 6"
Overall length	20' 6", 20' 11" fitted	20' 11"
Width over side flaps	8' 4"	8' 4"
SR running numbers	39001 – 39350	39351 – 39450, 39651 – 39955
Departmental numbers	none known	none known
Internal user numbers	none known	none known
Examples extant	none known	none known

Although used predominantly for containers, these trucks (Conflat A unfitted and Conflat B fitted) could also be used to convey road vehicles (Conflat S).

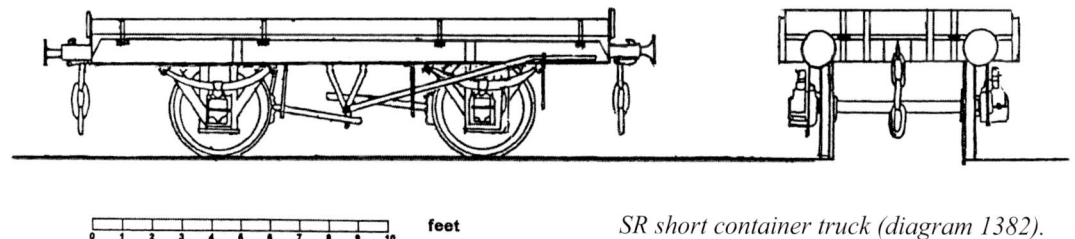

SR short container truck (diagram 1382). (Terry Gough)

SR short container truck number S39214 photographed at an unknown location, circa 1953. (Mike King Collection)

A PICTORIAL GUIDE TO SOUTHERN WAGONS AND VANS

SR short container truck number 39035 photographed pre-1948. (British Railways)

SR container truck (long)

Built by or for	SR
SR diagram number	1383
Description	14-ton or 15-ton container truck (long), Conflat C and D (vacuum braked)
Quantity built	150
Date	1931 – 1933
Quantity at Nationalisation	all
Underframe material	steel
Wheelbase	18' 7"
Length over headstocks	29' 0"
Overall length	32' 0" unfitted or 32' 5" fitted
Width over side flaps	8' 4"
Height above rails	4' 9½"
SR running numbers	39501 – 39650
SR running numbers (passenger van stock)	4207 ex 39582, 4208 ex 39614
Departmental number (example)	ADS39634
Internal user numbers (examples)	083635 ex ADS39555, 083627 ex 39617
Examples extant	39613 39617 39634
Location	SwanageR BluebellR SwanageR

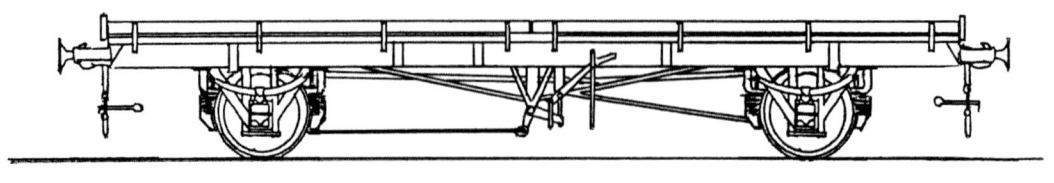

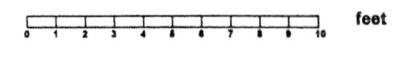

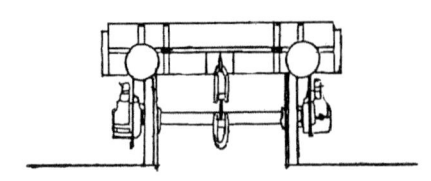

SR long container truck (diagram 1383). (Terry Gough)

TRUCKS

Above: SR long container truck number ADS39634 photographed at Norden on 10th August 2005. (Terry Gough)

Right: Detail from container truck. (Terry Gough)

SR/BR BD type container

Built by or for	SR/LMSR	BR
SR diagram number	3026	3/051
Description	4-ton container BD type	5-ton
Quantity built by SR	14	–
Quantity built by BR	–	205
Date	1944/45	1949
Quantity at Nationalisation	all	–
Body material	plywood	plywood
Body length	16' 0"	16' 0"
Overall length	16' 6"	16' 6"
Body width	7' 0"	7' 0"
Width over fenders	7' 6"	7' 6"
Height	7' 11½"	8' 0"
SR running numbers	BD1218 – 1231	BD4225B – 4299B, BD4365B – 4494B
Examples extant	none known	

There were thousands of containers and many different versions, both in SR and BR days. Some were for conveyance of general merchandise, others for specific types of traffic such as meat, eggs or even bicycles. Containers, many in very poor condition, are still to be found in railway and other locations across the country, but as far as is known, all are of BR origin.

General merchandise containers (known as type BD) usually had doors on both sides, and at one end only. The SR built containers were almost all of plywood construction, as were a few almost identical containers built by BR to diagram 3/051. However, by far the majority built by BR had tongue and groove timber bodies. Metal strapping was virtually the same on both the SR containers to diagram 3026 and the BR containers illustrated. An SR container to diagram 3026 is shown on page 76.

A PICTORIAL GUIDE TO SOUTHERN WAGONS AND VANS

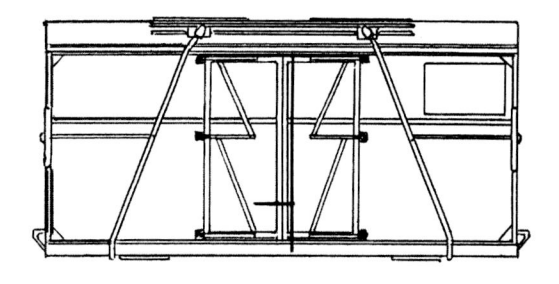

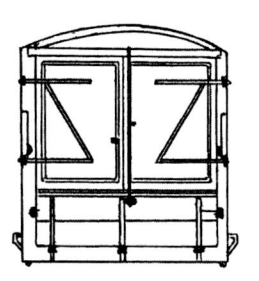

SR/BR BD type container (diagram 3026). (Terry Gough)

*Unidentified BR BD type container photographed at Didcot on 14th July 2005.
(Terry Gough)*

Unidentified BR BD type containers photographed at Didcot on 21st January 2006. (Terry Gough)

78

TRUCKS

SR/BR BK and B type containers

Built by or for	SR	BR
SR diagram number	3028	3/049
Description	4-ton container BK type	B type
Quantity built	25	325
Date	1947	1956/57
Quantity at Nationalisation	all	–
Body material	plywood	plywood/pressed steel
Body length	16' 0"	16' 0"
Overall length	16' 6"	16' 5"
Body width	7' 0"	7' 0"
Width over fenders	7' 6"	7' 5"
Height	7' 11½"	7' 11½"
Running numbers	BK1314 – 1338	B55525B – 55849B
Examples extant	none known	B55730B
Location		SevernR

These containers were designed to carry furniture. The only doors were at one end. Sides and ends were all plywood. The nearest BR equivalent containers were to diagrams 3/125, 3/126 and 3/127. There were also BR general merchandise containers type B to diagram 3/049, some of which had plywood bodies. Apart from having one end constructed in corrugated pressed steel, they were externally almost identical to the furniture containers. Pressed steel ends were very common on BR containers of most types, but unusual on the SR.

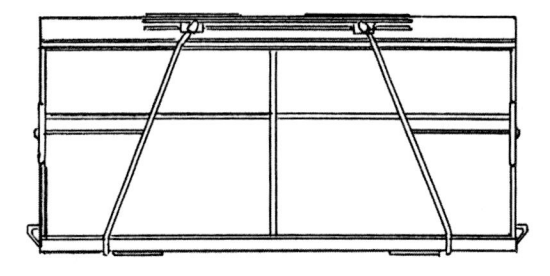

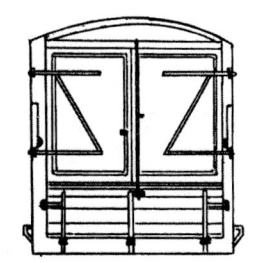

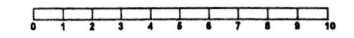

SR BK type container (diagram 3028). (Terry Gough)

BR B type container number B55730B photographed at Bewdley on 24th September 2005. (Terry Gough)

79

SR K and BK type container

Built by or for	SR	SR
SR diagram number	3011	3018
Description	4-ton container K type	BK type
Quantity built	50	77
Date	1932	1936 – 1943
Quantity at Nationalisation	all	all
Body material	armoured plywood	armoured plywood
Body length	15' 3"	15' 3"
Overall length	15' 7"	15' 7"
Body width	7' 0"	7' 0"
Width over fenders	7' 3"	7' 3"
Height	8' 3"	8' 0"
SR running numbers	K590 – 639	BK793 – 815

The first batch was built for furniture removals, later batches also for general merchandise. They all had doors at one end only.

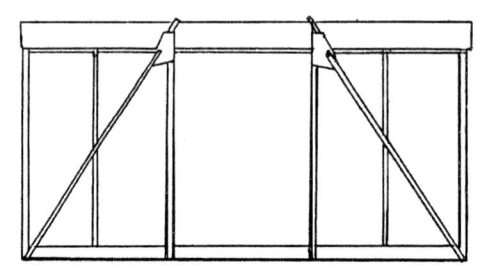

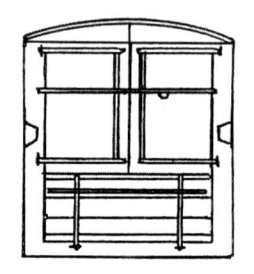

SR K and BK type container (diagrams 3011 and 3018). (Terry Gough)

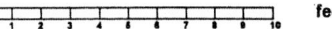

These three views were taken on 7th July 2006, on non-railway property near Keighley and show a container that has no identifying marks but is visually almost identical to containers built to these two diagrams. (Terry Gough)

CHAPTER 2
ENGINEERS' VEHICLES

Track relaying at Surbiton on 18th February 1962. In the foreground are two Borail wagons. To the left is an SR brake van on a train of Grampus/Lamprey ballast wagons. On the far right is Class U No 31621 on another train of Grampus wagons. In the centre of all this activity is a down Portsmouth train of 4-COR units on the up line. (Terry Gough)

Woking engineers' yard on 8th March 1969. In the foreground is SR bogie bolster No 58038, built to diagram 1599. (Terry Gough)

81

A PICTORIAL GUIDE TO SOUTHERN WAGONS AND VANS

Brake Vans

SECR/SR/BR ballast plough brake vans

Built by or for	SECR/SR	BR
SR diagram number	1748	1749
Description	20-ton ballast plough brake vans (BR Shark)	
Quantity built	4	8
Date	1914, 1932	1949
Quantity at Nationalisation	all	–
Underframe material	steel	steel
Wheelbase	18' 0"	18' 0"
Body length	25' 0"	25' 0"
Overall length	28' 6"	28' 6"
Body width	7' 8"	7' 8"
Height above rails	11' 3"	11' 3"
SR running numbers (examples)	62030 – 62032, 62523	62857 – 62864
Departmental numbers	all DS	all DS
Internal user numbers	none	none
Examples extant	DS62523	62861 62862 62864
Location	MidlandC	ChasewaterR KESR BluebellR

It seems amazing that a design of 1914 should be adopted by BR virtually unchanged.

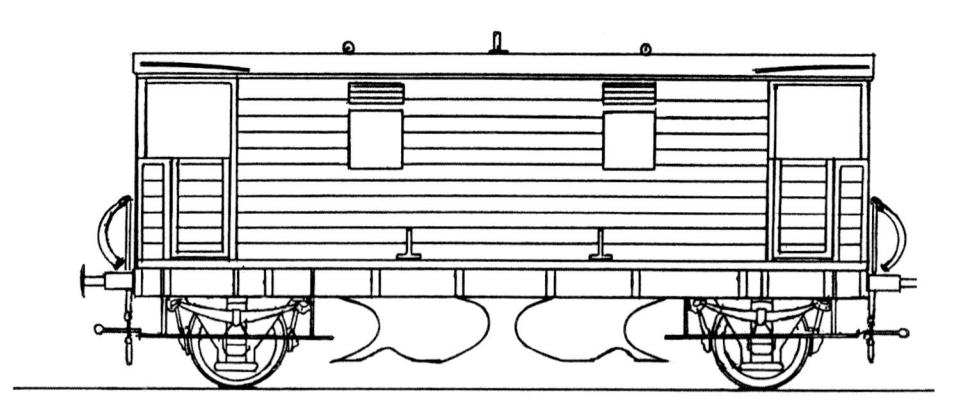

SECR ballast plough brake van (diagram 1749). (Terry Gough)

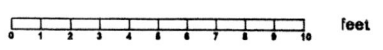

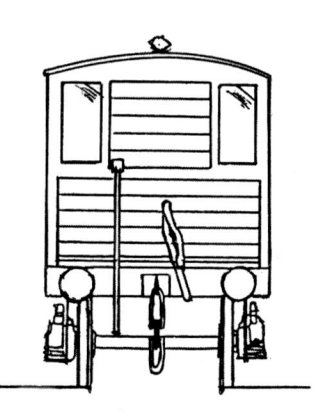

SECR ballast plough brake van number DS62863 photographed at Woking in May 1970. (Terry Gough)

BRAKE VANS

Detail from SECR ballast plough brake van number DS62863 photographed at Woking in May 1970. (Terry Gough)

SECR/BR ballast brake van

Built by or for	SECR/BR
SR diagram number	1761 ex 1560
Description	25-ton ballast brake van
Quantity built	10
Date converted	1953
Underframe material	steel
Wheelbase	16' 0"
Body length	24' 0"
Overall length	27' 0"
Body width	7' 10"
Height above rails	12' 0"
SR running numbers (examples)	55492 – 55494
Departmental numbers	all DS
Internal user numbers	none
Examples extant	none known

This is another SECR design, in this instance from a goods brake van, converted by BR. It was not a plough brake van, but was used as a permanent way staff riding van as well as a ballast brake van. See diagram 1560 (page 48) for a drawing of the veranda end of the van.

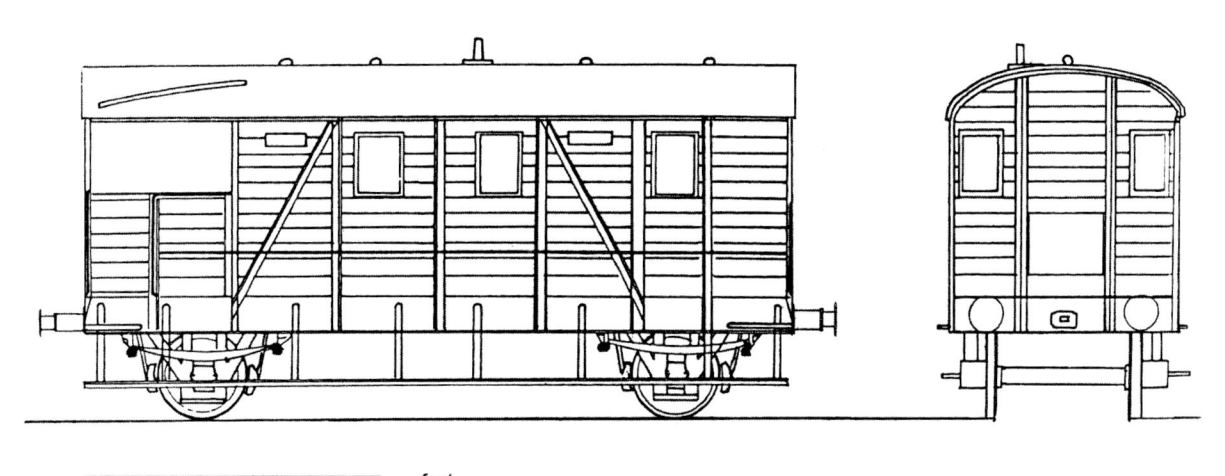

SECR/BR ballast brake van (diagram 1761). (Terry Gough)

83

A PICTORIAL GUIDE TO SOUTHERN WAGONS AND VANS

SECR/BR ballast brake van number DS55476 photographed at Woking in August 1965. (Terry Gough)

LBSCR/SR ballast brake van

Built by or for	LBSCR/SR
SR diagram number	1760 ex 1576
Description	20-ton ballast brake van
Quantity built	17
Date converted	1928 – 1937
Quantity at Nationalisation	16
Underframe material	steel
Wheelbase	16' 0"
Body length	24' 0"
Overall length	27' 0"
Body width	8' 0"
Height above rails	11' 9"
SR running numbers (examples)	62840 – 62856
Departmental numbers	all
Internal user numbers	none
Examples extant	none

These goods brake vans were converted by the SR for use as ballast brake vans and for permanent way staff. Note the different body side materials on the two vans illustrated. See diagram 1576 (page 50) for a drawing of the veranda end of the van.

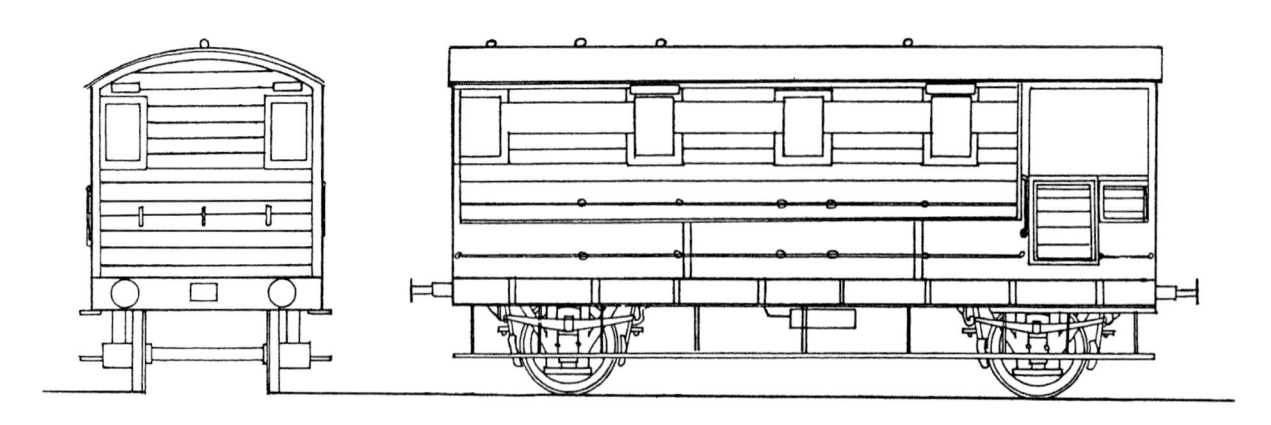

LBSCR/SR ballast brake van (diagram 1760). (Terry Gough)

84

BRAKE VANS

LBSCR/SR ballast brake van number DS62845 photographed at Woking on 11th August 1965. (Terry Gough)

LBSCR/SR ballast brake van number DS62845 photographed at Woking on 11th August 1965. (Terry Gough)

LBSCR/SR ballast brake van number DS62855 photographed at Woking on 30th April 1966. (Terry Gough)

A PICTORIAL GUIDE TO SOUTHERN WAGONS AND VANS

Ballast Wagons

Meldon Quarry was an obvious place to see ballast wagons, and on 7th July 1961 ex LSWR Class O2 No DS682 shunts several wagons in the yard. The first three wagons are all to SR designs that were perpetuated by BR. (Terry Gough)

A train of bogie hoppers from Woking enters Betchworth behind SR Class S15 No 30847 on 28th April 1962. (Terry Gough)

BALLAST WAGONS

SECR/BR ballast hopper

Built by or for	SECR	BR
SR diagram number	1746	1/584
Description	20-ton ballast hopper	20-ton Herring
Quantity built	7	100
Date	1915	1952
Quantity at Nationalisation	probably all	–
Underframe material	steel	steel
Wheelbase	12' 6"	13' 0"
Hopper length	18' 1"	17' 3"
Length over headstocks	21' 0"	21' 8"
Overall length	24' 6"	24' 8"
Body width	7' 11"	8' 4"
Height above rails	8' 1½"	8' 0"
SR/BR running numbers	62494 – 62500	992381 – 480
Departmental numbers	all DS	all DB
Internal user numbers	none known	none known
Examples extant	none	DB992387 DB992447
Location		LlangollenR GCR

The hopper is asymmetrically placed on the chassis to give access to the hopper discharge control mechanism at one end of the wagon.

This small order by the SECR did not result in any further vehicles of this type being purchased by the SR. Some were, however, built for the LMSR and LNER in 1926. Remarkably the design was adopted with minor modifications by BR, resulting in over 200 vehicles being built. There are only minor visual differences. Unlike the SECR hoppers, there is no small drop door on the upper part of the hopper side. The SECR wagons (and those to the BR Trout, diagram 1/580) have three discharge control wheels, whereas on the Mackerel (diagram 1/583) and Herring (1/584), there is only one wheel. Some Mackerel and Herring were retrofitted with roller bearings.

Above: BR Herring number DB992447 photographed at Quorn on 23rd June 2006. (Terry Gough)

Left: Interior view of BR Herring number DB992447 photographed at Quorn on 23rd June 2006. (Terry Gough)

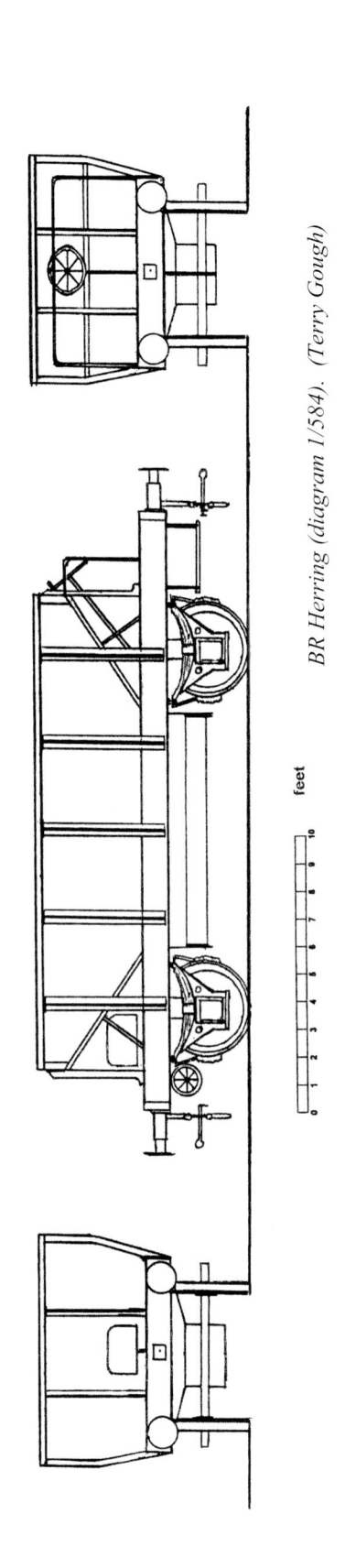

A PICTORIAL GUIDE TO SOUTHERN WAGONS AND VANS

BR Herring (diagram 1/584). (Terry Gough)

Two views of end detail of BR Herring number DB992447 photographed at Quorn on 23rd June 2006. (Terry Gough)

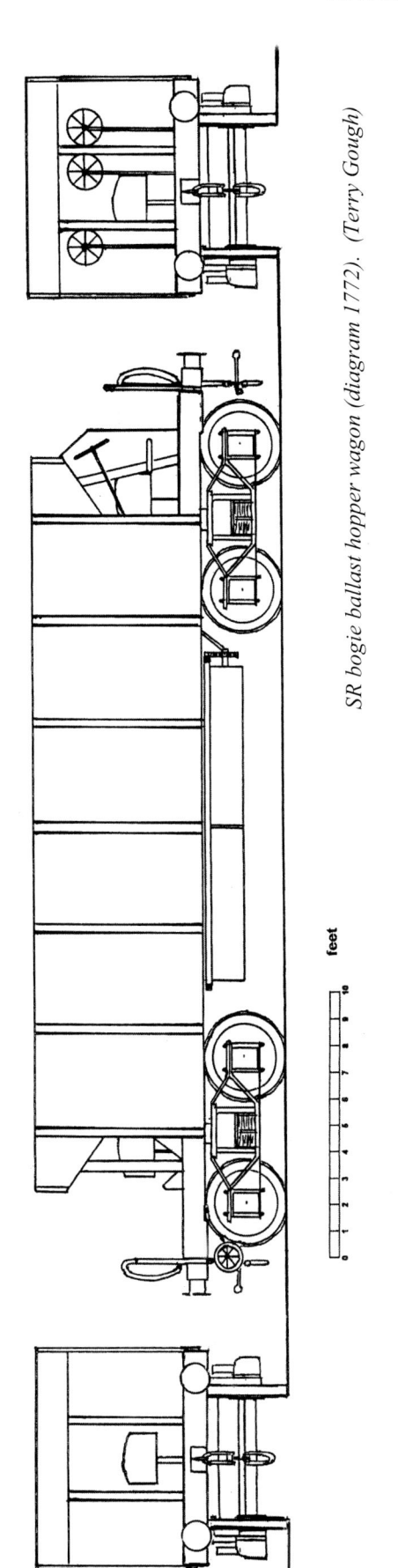

BALLAST WAGONS

SR bogie ballast hopper wagon (diagram 1772). (Terry Gough)

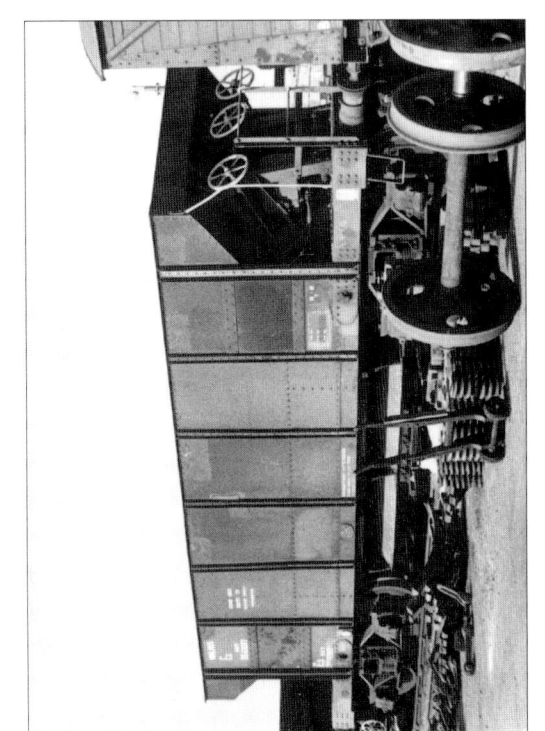

SR bogie ballast hopper wagon number DS62017 photographed at Woking on 8th March 1969. (Terry Gough)

SR bogie ballast hopper wagons

Built by or for	SR	SR	SR
SR diagram number	1772	1774	1775
Description	40-ton bogie ballast hopper wagons (BR Walrus)		
Quantity built	25	22	20
Date	1928/29	1936/37	1947
Quantity at Nationalisation	probably all	probably all	all
Underframe material	steel	steel	steel
Bogie centres	23' 0"	23' 0"	23' 0"
Bogie type	LSWR/SR	LSWR/SR	SR cast
Wheelbase	5' 6"	5' 6"	5' 6"
Hopper length	27' 10"	27' 10"	27' 11"
Length over headstocks	32' 6"	32' 6"	32' 6"
Overall length	35' 6"	35' 6"	35' 6"
Hopper width	8' 4"	8' 4"	8' 4"
Height above rails	9' 9"	9' 9"	9' 9"
SR/BR running numbers	62005 – 62029	62033 – 62054	62055 – 62074
Departmental numbers	all	all	all
Internal user numbers	none known	none known	none known
Examples extant		62041	62064 62070
Location		WorthR	MoorsR SwanageR

Wagons to diagram 1772 have hopper discharge controls at one end only, whereas wagons to diagrams 1774 and 1775 have controls at both ends. Diagram 1772 wagons have shallower ballast chutes than those of subsequent diagrams. Note also the two different types of bogie.

BR also built wagons developed from diagram 1775 and these are still in use on the National Network.

Above: SR bogie ballast hopper wagon number 62070 photographed at Norden on 13th December 2005.

Right: End detail of the above.
(Both Terry Gough)

BALLAST WAGONS

Above: Discharge detail from SR bogie ballast hopper wagon number 62070.

Right: Bogie detail from SR bogie ballast hopper wagon number 62070. (Both Terry Gough)

SR 5-plank ballast dropside wagon

Built by or for	SR
SR diagram number	1771
Description	20-ton 5-plank ballast dropside wagon
Quantity built	60
Date	1928
Quantity at Nationalisation	probably all
Underframe material	steel
Wheelbase	12' 0"
Body length	21' 6"
Overall length	24' 6"
Body width	8' 0"
Height above rails	7' 0"
SR running numbers	61945 – 62004
Departmental numbers	probably all
Internal user numbers	several to Western Region at Swindon
Examples extant	DS61953 DS61989 62002
Location	GCR SwanageR BluebellR

All wagons were fitted.

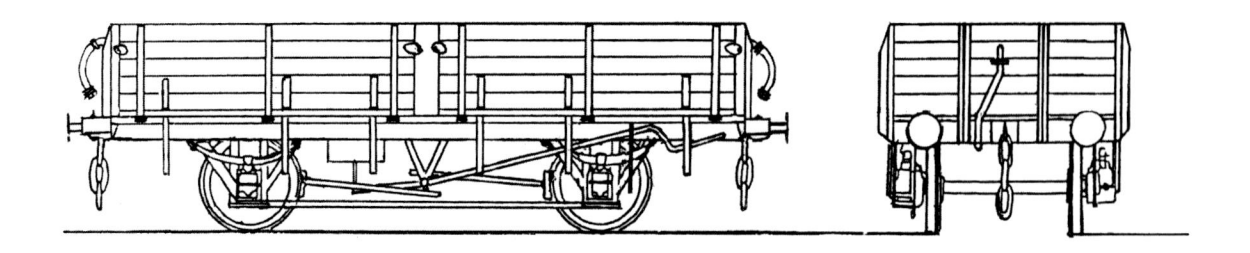

SR 5-plank ballast dropside wagon (diagram 1771). (Terry Gough)

Above: SR 5-plank ballast dropside wagon number DS61985 photographed at Woking on 2nd August 1969. (Terry Gough)

Left: SR 5-plank ballast dropside wagon number 61989 photographed at Norden on 13th December 2005. (Terry Gough)

BALLAST WAGONS

SR 4-plank ballast dropside wagon

Built by or for	SR
SR diagram number	1773
Description	15-ton 4-plank ballast dropside wagon
Quantity built	50
Date	1937
Quantity at Nationalisation	probably all
Underframe material	steel
Wheelbase	12' 0"
Body length	21' 6"
Overall length	24' 6"
Body width	8' 0"
Height above rails	6' 5"
SR running numbers	63001 – 63050
Departmental numbers	probably all
Internal user numbers	083499 ex ADS63044, 083526 ex ADS63045
Examples extant	none known

These wagons are a lower capacity and unfitted version of wagons to diagram 1771 (page 91).

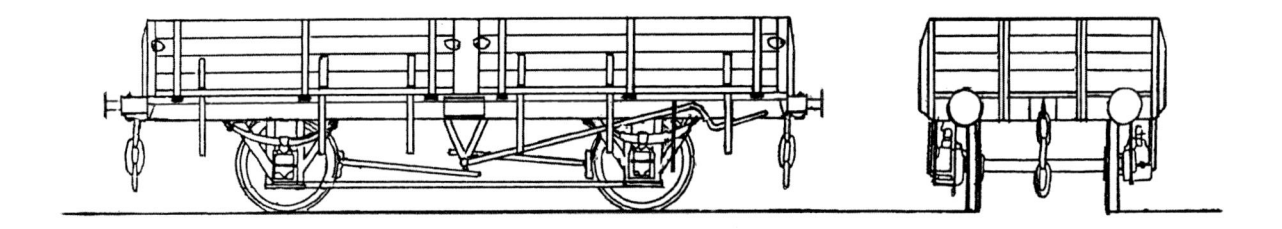

SR 4-plank ballast dropside wagon (diagram 1773). (Terry Gough)

SR 4-plank ballast dropside wagon number DS63026 photographed at Woking on 2nd August 1969. (Terry Gough)

93

A PICTORIAL GUIDE TO SOUTHERN WAGONS AND VANS

SR/BR steel-sided ballast dropside wagon

Built by or for	SR/BR
BR diagram number	1/570
Description	20-ton steel-sided ballast dropside wagon (BR Lamprey)
Quantity built	231
Date	1951/52
Underframe material	steel
Wheelbase	12' 0"
Body length	21' 6"
Overall length	24' 11"
Body width	9' 0"
Height above rails	6' 9"
BR running numbers	DB991141 – 991300
Departmental numbers	all
Internal user number	none known
Example extant	DB991235
Location	DartR

These wagons were designed by Bulleid in 1945 for ballast and sleepers, but not built until after Nationalisation. Both the sides and ends were hinged to drop, 2 flaps on each side and one at each end. DB991295 shown in the photograph was built as a Lamprey, but when photographed in 1969 was marked as Grampus. Wagons built to diagram 1/574 (Grampus) had lower body sides, three drop doors per side and one each end.

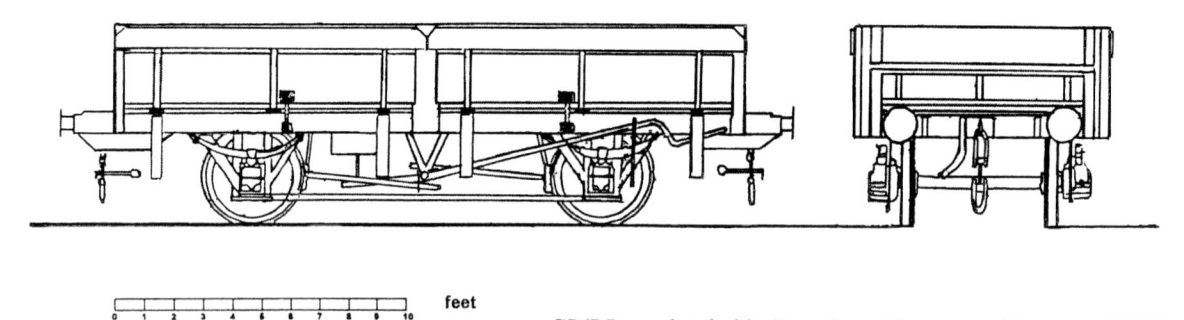

SR/BR steel-sided ballast dropside wagon (diagram 1/570). (Terry Gough)

SR/BR steel-sided ballast dropside wagon number DB991295 photographed at Woking on 8th March 1969. (Terry Gough)

CHAPTER 3

PASSENGER VANS

An up vans train passes Surbiton behind Class U No 31627 on 2nd September 1962. The first three vehicles are all of SR origin, being a 4-wheeled luggage brake van, a bogie luggage brake van and a 4-wheeled luggage van. (Terry Gough)

A row of condemned vans at Barry on 25th August 1981, almost all of which are SR. (Terry Gough)

A PICTORIAL GUIDE TO SOUTHERN WAGONS AND VANS

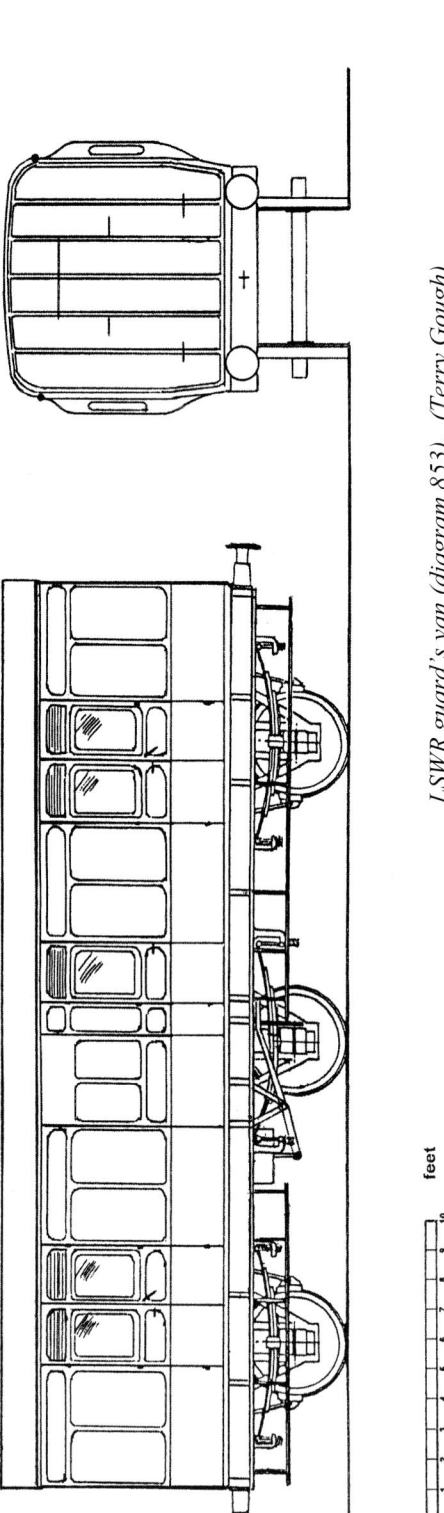

LSWR guard's van (diagram 853). (Terry Gough)

Model of LSWR guard's van (diagram 853). (Terry Gough)

LSWR guard's van number 874s photographed at Wadebridge on 5th July 1948. (J H Aston)

96

GUARD'S VANS

Guard's Vans

LSWR guard's van

Built by or for	LSWR
SR diagram number	853
Description	11-ton guard's van
Quantity built	65
Date	1892 – 1897
Quantity at Nationalisation	1 on IOW, and several in Departmental use
Underframe material	timber
Wheelbase	10' 0" + 10' 0"
Body length	30' 0"
Overall length	33' 7"
Body width	8' 1", 9' 1" over duckets
Height above rails	12' 0"
SR running numbers (examples)	83 – 101, IOW 1002 ex 44, 1003 ex 62
Departmental numbers (examples)	874s ex 39, 949s ex 81, DS1345(s) ex 86, 913s ex 97
Internal user numbers	none
Examples extant	none

Both sides of the van were identical.

LSWR guard's van

Built by or for	LSWR
SR diagram number	870
Description	bogie guard's van
Original building date	1908
Date of first rebuild	1917
Date of second rebuild	circa 1920
Quantity rebuilt	4
Quantity at Nationalisation	3
Underframe material	steel
Bogie centres	39' 0"
Wheelbase	8' 0"
Body length	56' 0"
Overall length	59' 7"
Body width	8' 7", 9' 1" over duckets
Height above rails	12' 0"
SR running numbers	327 – 329, 345
Departmental numbers	DS223(s) ex 327, DS3177 ex 328, DS447(s) ex 345
Internal user numbers	none
Examples extant	none

Four LSWR brake thirds were converted into ambulance vehicles, which in turn were converted into luggage/guard's vans to this diagram. There were similar vehicles, some with centre duckets, converted from other LSWR brake thirds and thirds. For photographs of bogies, see under diagram 3098 (page 119).

A PICTORIAL GUIDE TO SOUTHERN WAGONS AND VANS

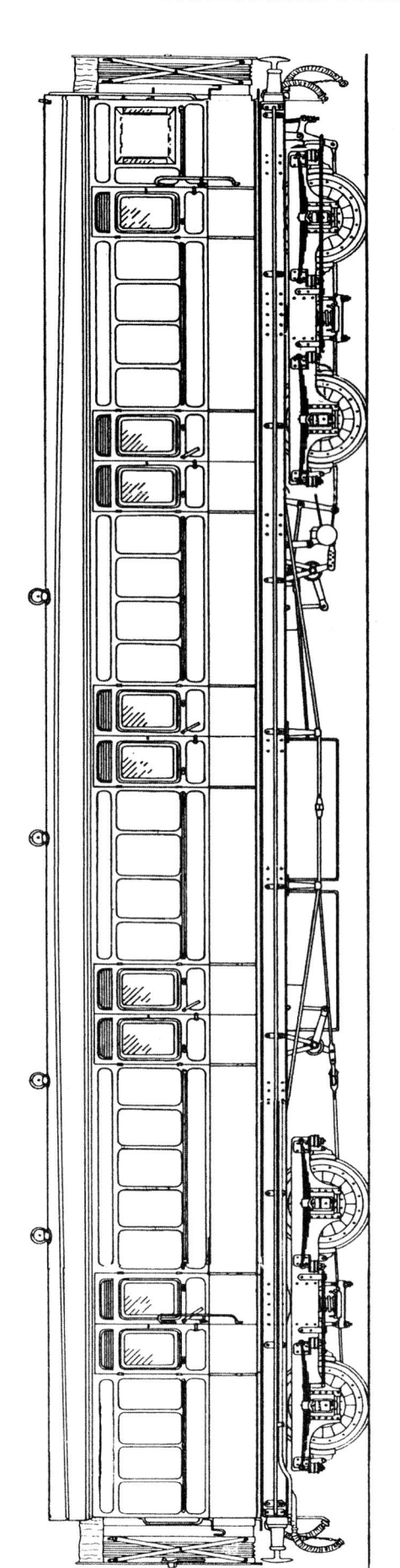

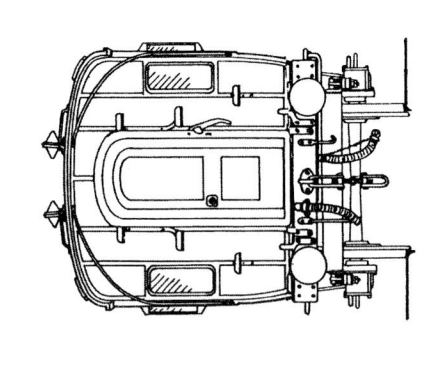

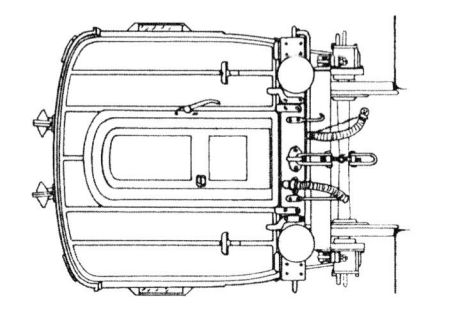

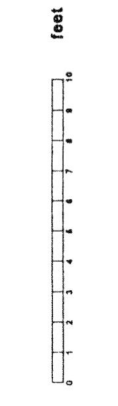

LSWR guard's van (diagram 870). (Gordon Weddell)

LSWR guard's van number DS447 photographed possibly at Strawberry Hill on an unknown date. (John Smith)

GUARD'S VANS

Above: LSWR guard's van number DS3177 photographed at Lancing post-1948. (John Smith)

Left: Model of LSWR guard's van. (diagram 870). (Terry Gough)

LSWR guard's van

Built by or for   LSWR
SR diagram number   863
Description   8-ton bogie guard's van
Approximate quantity built   160
Date   1893 – 1902
Quantity at Nationalisation   10
Underframe material   timber
Bogie centres   various (27' 9", 28' 3", 29' 3")
Wheelbase   8' 0"
Body length   44' 0"
Overall length   47' 8"
Body width   8'1", 9' 1" over duckets
Height above rails   12' 0"
SR running numbers   272 – 286, IOW 1014 ex 185, 1015 ex 280
Departmental numbers   none known
Internal user numbers   none
Examples extant   none

Battery boxes were on the other side on the IOW vehicles.

A PICTORIAL GUIDE TO SOUTHERN WAGONS AND VANS

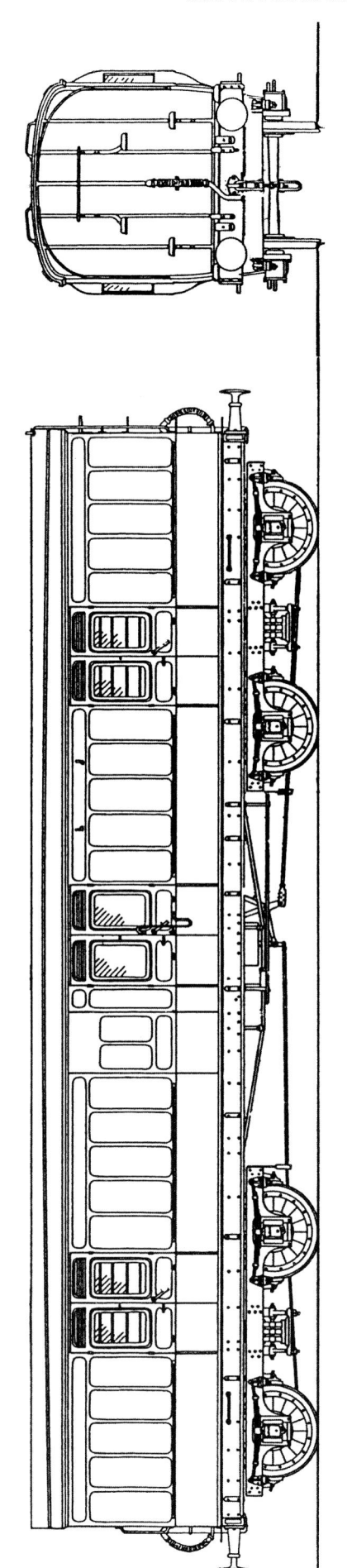

LSWR bogie guard's van (diagram 863). (Gordon Weddell)

LSWR bogie detail. (Terry Gough)

LSWR bogie guard's van number S1014 photographed at Ryde Pier Head, post-1948. (John Smith)

100

GUARD'S VANS

Model of LSWR bogie guard's van (diagram 863). (Terry Gough)

SER/SECR guard's van

Built by or for	SER/SECR
SR diagram number	884
Description	13-ton guard's van
Approximate quantity built	26
Date	1886 – 1901
Quantity at Nationalisation	3, all as Departmental vehicles
Underframe material	timber
Wheelbase	9' 9" + 9' 9"
Body length	32' 0"
Overall length	35' 9"
Body width	7' 1", 8' 4" over duckets
Height above rails	11' 10"
SR running numbers (examples)	523 – 548
Departmental numbers (examples)	DS1536(s) ex 524, DS1510(s) ex 529, DS870(s) ex 540
Internal user numbers	none
Examples extant	none

The van had steps at one end only. For axlebox and suspension detail see under diagram 1156 (page 125).
This van is illustrated on page 102.

SECR guard's van

Built by or for	SECR
SR diagram number	885
Description	13-ton guard's van
Quantity built	79
Date	1902, 1906
Quantity at Nationalisation	44, all as Departmental vehicles
Underframe material	timber
Wheelbase	9' 9" + 9' 9"
Body length	32' 0"
Overall length	35' 11"
Body width	7' 3", 8' 4" over duckets
Height above rails	12' 9" (including birdcage)
SR running numbers (examples)	611 – 630
Departmental numbers (examples)	DS1613(s) ex 597, DS1601(s) ex 616, DS1311(s) ex 628
Internal user numbers	none
Example extant	616
Location	BluebellR

The other side of the van is a mirror image, that is, the single door is to the left of the ducket.
For axlebox and suspension detail see under diagram 1156 (page 125).
This van is illustrated on page 103.

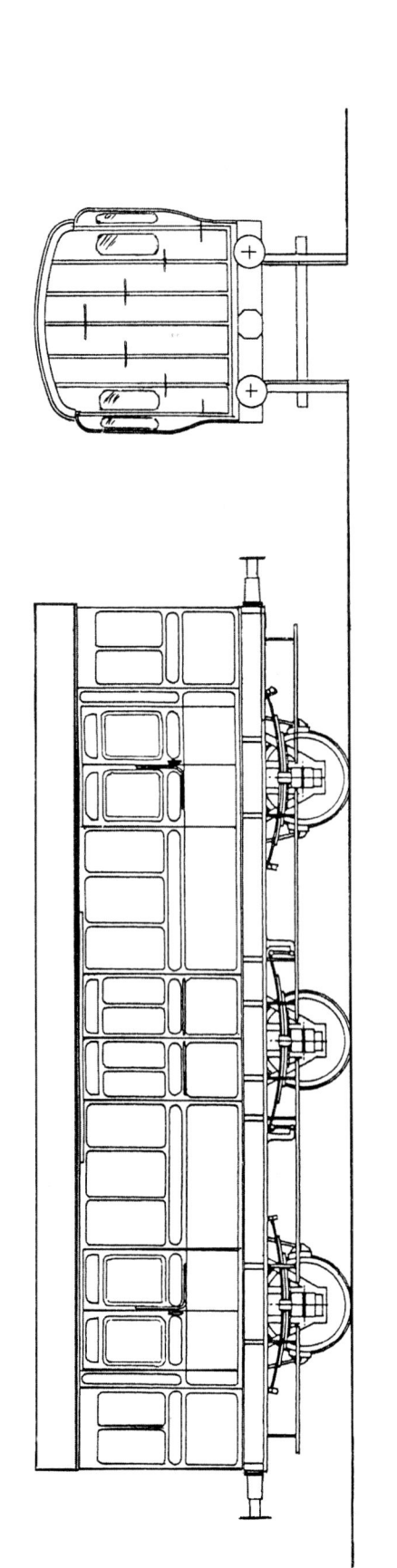

A PICTORIAL GUIDE TO SOUTHERN WAGONS AND VANS

SER/SECR guard's van (diagram 884). (Terry Gough)

Model of SER/SECR guard's van number 532 (diagram 884). (Terry Gough)

SER/SECR guard's van number 870s photographed at Exmouth Junction on 29th June 1948. (J H Aston)

102

GUARD'S VANS

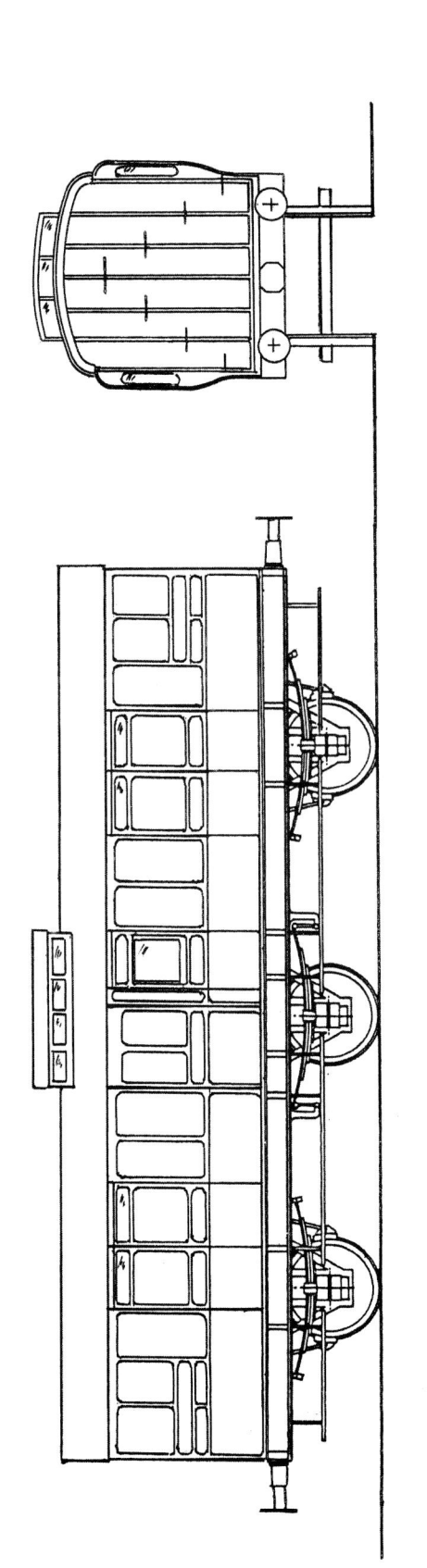

SECR guard's van (diagram 885). (Terry Gough)

Model of SECR guard's van (diagram 885). (Terry Gough)

Unnumbered SECR guard's van (ex 1601s) photographed at Chasewater in August 1969. (Terry Gough)

A PICTORIAL GUIDE TO SOUTHERN WAGONS AND VANS

Detail from unnumbered SECR guard's van (ex 1601s) photographed at Chasewater in August 1969. (Terry Gough)

SECR/SR guard's van

Built by or for	SECR/SR
SR diagram number	891
Description	bogie guard's van
Original building date	1911
Date of first rebuild	1924, 1926
Date of second rebuild	1956, 1957
Quantity rebuilt	4
Underframe material	steel
Bogie centres	38' 0"
Wheelbase	8' 0"
Body length	54' 1"
Overall length	57' 10"
Body width	8' 1"
Height above rails	11' 9"
SR running numbers	1013 – 1016 ex IOW 4138 – 4141, previously mainland 3394, 3396, 3398, 3399
Departmental numbers	none
Internal user numbers	none
Examples extant	none

These vans were rebuilt from SECR brake third coaches, specifically for the IOW. They were originally 7-compartment brake composites, rebuilt as 4-compartment brake thirds for use on the IOW.

SECR/SR guard's van number S1015 photographed at Newport on 12th August 1965. (Terry Gough)

GUARD'S VANS

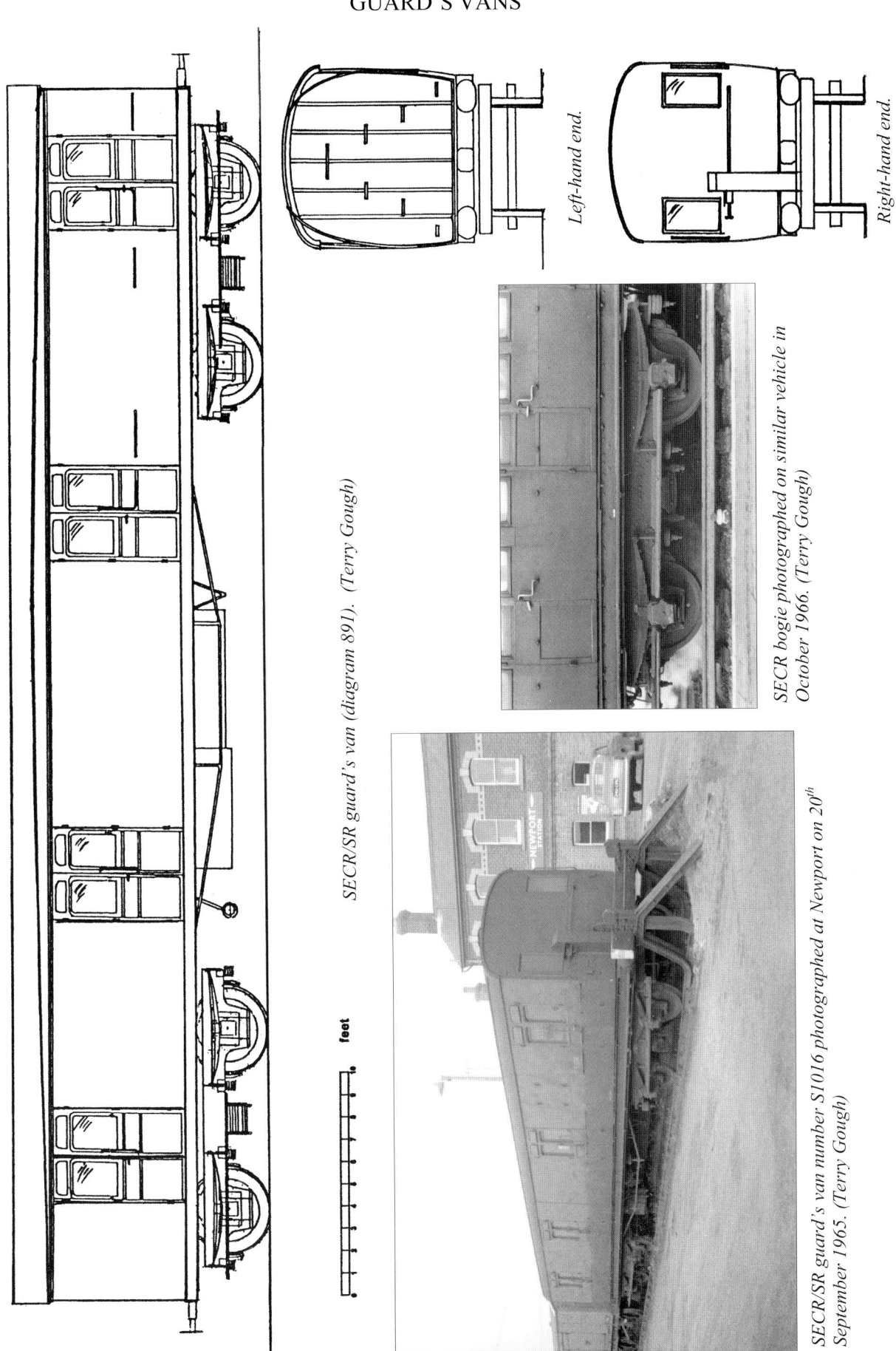

Left-hand end.

Right-hand end.

SECR/SR guard's van (diagram 891). (Terry Gough)

SECR bogie photographed on similar vehicle in October 1966. (Terry Gough)

SECR/SR guard's van number S1016 photographed at Newport on 20th September 1965. (Terry Gough)

SR Channel Ferry guard's van

Built by or for	SR
SR diagram number	3091
Description	17-ton Channel Ferry guard's van
Quantity built	3
Date	1936
Quantity at Nationalisation	all
Underframe material	steel
Wheelbase	23' 0"
Body length	36' 0"
Overall length	39' 8"
Body width	7' 10"
Height above rails	11' 7" (12' 8" with birdcage roof)
SR running numbers	1 – 3
Departmental numbers	none
Internal user numbers	none
Examples extant	none

It seems extraordinary that long after the SECR abandoned birdcage guard's lookouts, the SR should reintroduce them. These vehicles were built specifically for the Night Ferry, but in later years they were used as ordinary luggage vans.

The two sides were not identical, as shown in the photographs. The guard's door was inset by 4½". All planking was 6½".

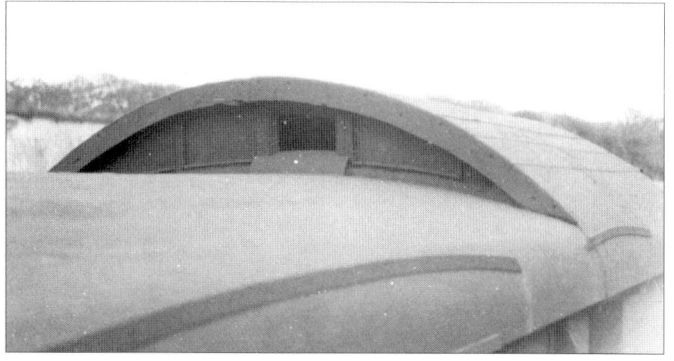

Above: SR Channel Ferry guard's van number S1S. (John Smith)

Left: Detail from SR Channel Ferry guard's van number S1S photographed at Micheldever in July 1970. (Terry Gough)

GUARD'S VANS

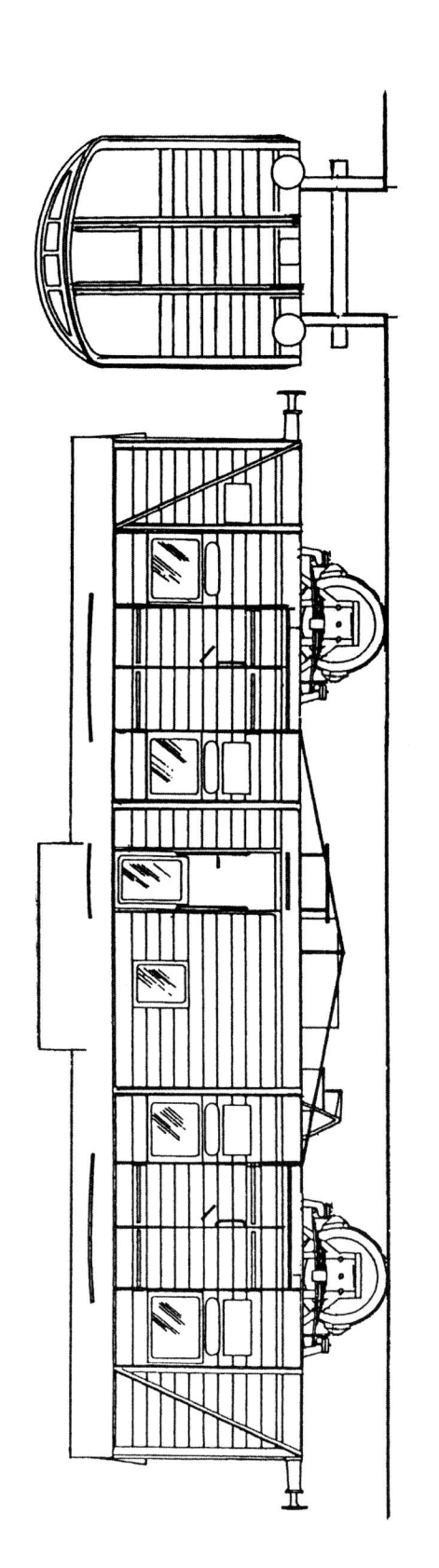

SR Channel Ferry guard's van (diagram 3091). (Terry Gough)

Three views of SR Channel Ferry guard's van number S3S photographed at Wimbledon on 28th November 1965. (Terry Gough)

A PICTORIAL GUIDE TO SOUTHERN WAGONS AND VANS

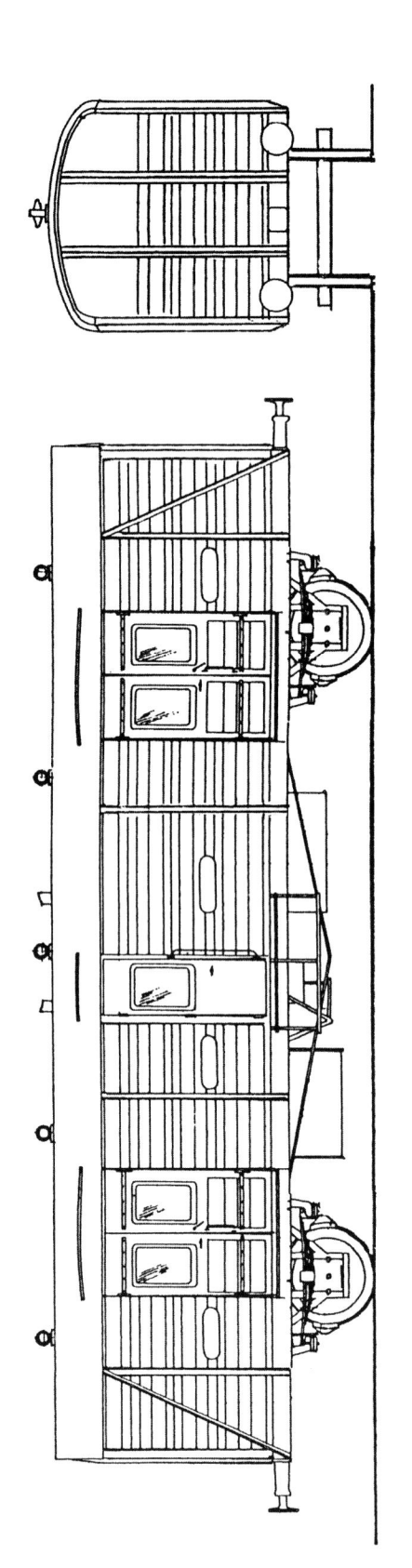

SR guard's van (diagram 3092). (Terry Gough)

Unidentified SR guard's van photographed at Clapham Junction in October 1968. (Terry Gough)

SR guard's van number S702S photographed at Walton on Thames on 5th July 1966. (Terry Gough)

GUARD'S VANS

SR guard's van

Built by or for	SR
SR diagram number	3092
Description	16-ton guard's van (SR Van C; BR BY)
Quantity built	250
Date	1937 – 1941
Quantity at Nationalisation	all
Underframe material	steel
Wheelbase	23' 0"
Body length	36' 0"
Overall length	39' 8"
Body width	7' 10"
Height above rails	12' 0"
SR running numbers (examples)	651 – 750
Departmental numbers (examples)	DS70323 ex 687, ADB975671 ex 746, DB975144 ex 964, KDB975143 ex 405
Internal user numbers (examples)	083356 ex 412, 083355 ex 699
Examples extant	404, 419, 442 405, 436
	BluebellR GwiliR

For axlebox details see under diagram 3103 (page 123).

Model of SR guard's van (diagram 3092). (Terry Gough)

SR/BR guard's van

Built by or for	SR/BR
SR diagram number	3093
Description	28-ton bogie guard's van (SR/BR; Van B)
Quantity built	130
Date	1939 – 1953
Quantity at Nationalisation	almost all
Underframe material	steel
Bogie centres	34' 10"
Wheelbase	8' 0"
Body length	50' 0"
Overall length	53' 8½"
Body width	7' 10"
Height above rails	12' 0"
SR running numbers (examples)	201 – 280
Departmental numbers (examples)	ADB977066 ex 249, TDB975402 ex 360
Internal user numbers (examples)	083618 ex 210, 083336 ex 379
Examples extant	201 210 273 392
Location	SpaR WightR MangappsR BodminR

All had wide/narrow pairs of planking. For end detail see under diagram 3092 (page 108). The vehicles photographed at Basingstoke and Woking were too dirty to discern their numbers.

A PICTORIAL GUIDE TO SOUTHERN WAGONS AND VANS

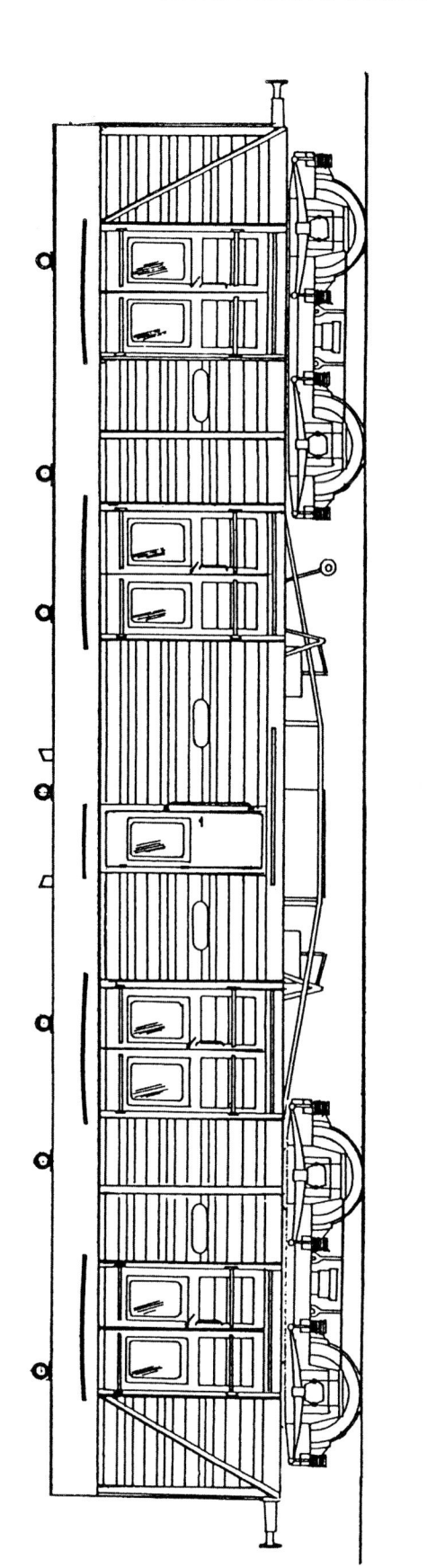

SR/BR guard's van (diagram 3093). (Terry Gough)

Unidentified SR/BR guard's van photographed at Basingstoke on 3rd July 1966.

Unidentified SR/BR guard's van photographed at Woking in 1981.

Ventilated Vans

LSWR ventilated or special milk van

Built by or for	LSWR
SR diagram number	932
Description	ventilated or special milk van
Quantity built	16
Date	1907 – 1909
Quantity at Nationalisation	4 (all Departmental)
Underframe material	timber
Wheelbase	10' 0" + 10' 0"
Body length	32' 0"
Overall length	35' 9"
Body width (over sliding doors)	8' 5"
Height above rails	11' 10½"
SR running numbers (examples)	1636 – 1642
Departmental numbers (examples)	DS1429(s) ex 1636, DS1414(s) ex 1642
Internal user numbers	none
Examples extant	none

Steps were only at one end of the body.

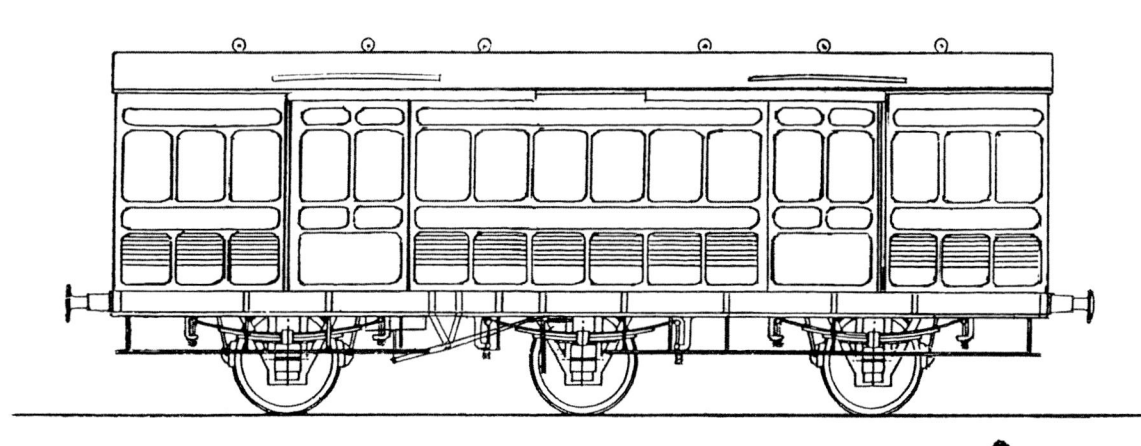

LSWR ventilated or special milk van (diagram 932). (Terry Gough)

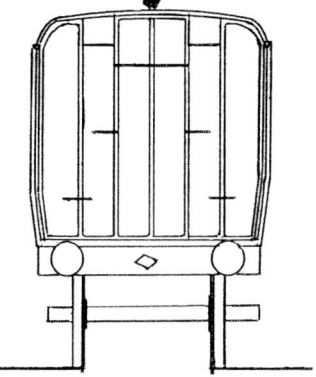

LSWR ventilated or special milk van number DS1414 photographed at Ashford post-1948. (John Smith)

A PICTORIAL GUIDE TO SOUTHERN WAGONS AND VANS

Above: LSWR ventilated or special milk van (ex 1640) photographed at Richmond on 3rd November 1965. (Terry Gough)

Left: Model of an LSWR ventilated or special milk van (diagram 932). (Terry Gough)

LSWR ventilated van (special luggage van)

Built by or for	LSWR
SR diagram number	929
Description	11-ton ventilated van (special luggage van)
Approximate quantity built	200
Date	1909 – 1923
Approximate quantity at Nationalisation	70 (all Departmental)
Underframe material	timber
Wheelbase	14' 0"
Body length	24' 0"
Overall length	27' 9"
Body width (over doors)	8' 5"
Height above rails	11' 8"
SR running numbers (examples)	1428 – 1481, 1584 – 1632
Departmental numbers (examples)	DS1446(s) ex 1475, DS1444(s) ex 1488, DS1686(s) ex 1584, DS1590(s) ex 1629
Internal user numbers	none
Examples extant	1451 1584
Location	BucksR BluebellR

Steps were only at one end of the body.

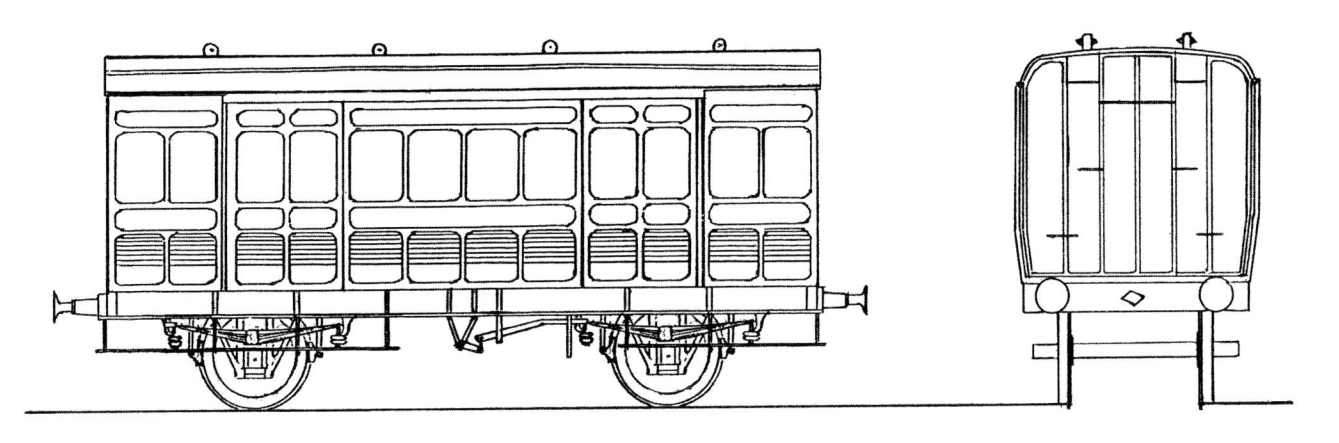

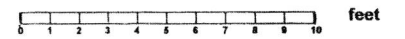

VENTILATED VANS

LSWR ventilated van (diagram 929). (Terry Gough)

Above: LSWR ventilated van number DS1686 photographed at Liss in April 1971. (Terry Gough)

Below: Details from the van pictured above.

A PICTORIAL GUIDE TO SOUTHERN WAGONS AND VANS

Above: Model of LSWR ventilated van number 1528 (diagram 929). (Terry Gough)

Left: LSWR ventilated van number 1451 photographed at Tisbury in September 1968. This view shows the opposite end to the van on the previous page. (Terry Gough)

LSWR bullion/specie van

Built by or for	LSWR
SR diagram number	940
Description	10-ton bogie bullion/specie van
Quantity built	12
Date	1911, 1912
Quantity at Nationalisation	10
Underframe material	steel
Bogie centres	29' 0"
Wheelbase	8' 0"
Body length	44' 0"
Overall length	47' 4"
Body width	8' 1"
Height above rails	12' 0"
SR running numbers	1680 – 1691
Departmental numbers (examples)	DS105 ex 1681, DS3170 ex 1685, DS109 ex 1689
Internal user numbers	none
Examples extant	none

For bogies, see under diagram 3098 (page 119). There are no steps at either end of the body.

Model of an LSWR bullion/specie van (diagram 940). (Terry Gough)

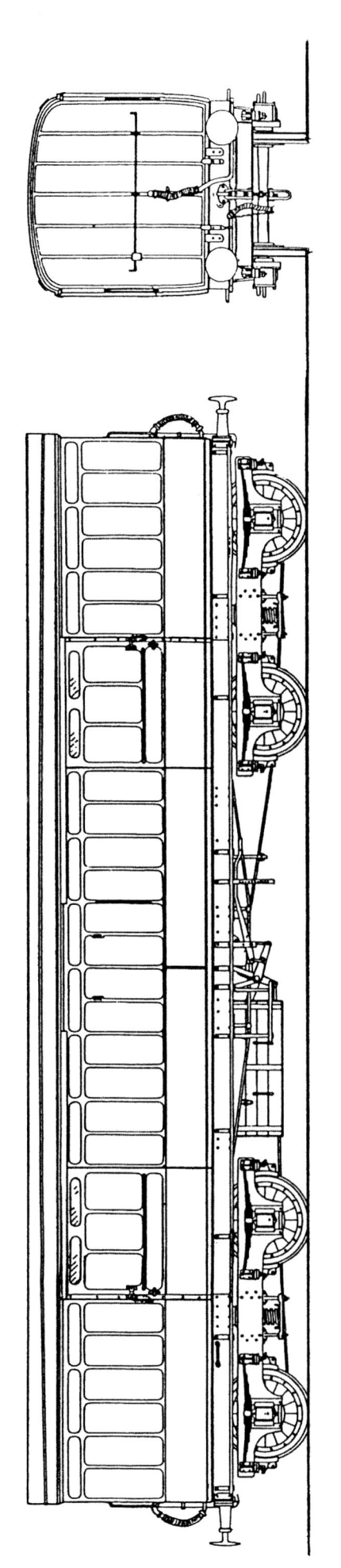

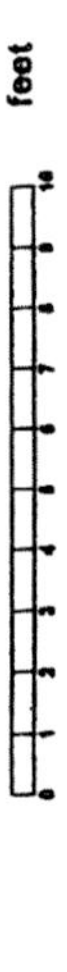

VENTILATED VANS

LSWR bullion/specie van (diagram 940). (Gordon Weddell)

LSWR bullion/specie van number DS109 photographed at Feltham on 14th June 1966. This view shows a bullion van made insecure by virtue of conversion to Departmental use. (Terry Gough)

LSWR bullion/specie van number S1688 photographed at Clapham Junction, post-1948. (John Smith)

115

A PICTORIAL GUIDE TO SOUTHERN WAGONS AND VANS

Luggage Vans

SECR luggage van

Built by or for	SECR
SR diagram number	960
Description	12/13-ton luggage van (SR PLV; BR PMV)
Quantity built	45
Date	1919 – 1922
Quantity at Nationalisation	almost all
Underframe material	steel 9" solebars
Wheelbase	21' 0"
Body length	32' 0"
Overall length	35' 10"
Body width	7' 10"
Height above rails	12' 0"
SR running numbers (examples)	1972 – 2016
Departmental numbers (examples)	DS251(s) ex 1991, DS70031 ex 1994, DS792 ex 1995
Internal user number (example)	082757 ex 1972
Examples extant	1972 DS70031
Location	KESR BluebellR

The forerunner of the standard SR luggage van. Body sides are constructed with 6½" planks.

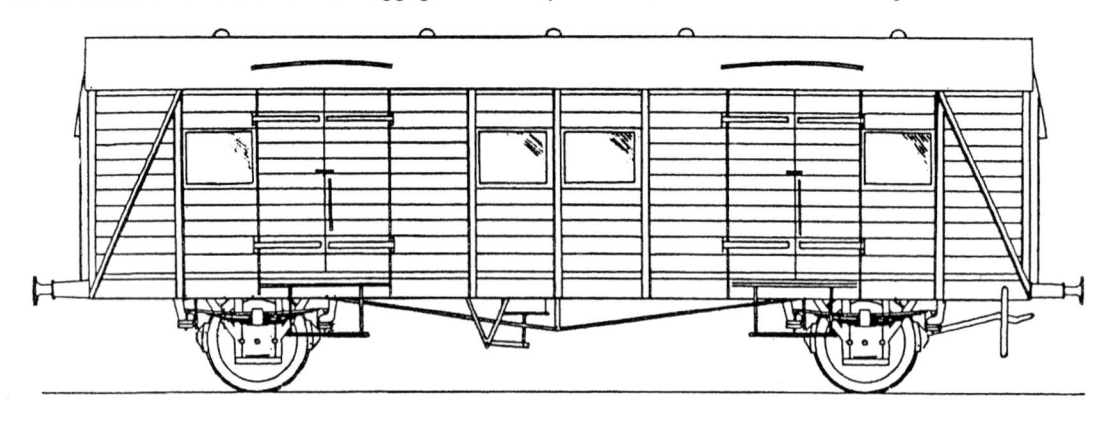

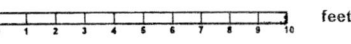

SECR luggage van (diagram 960). (Terry Gough)

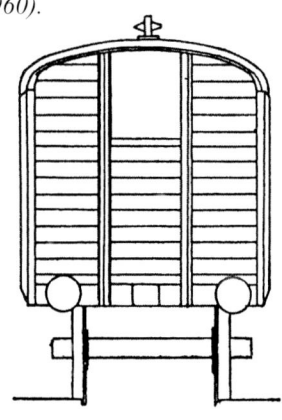

SECR luggage van number DS251 photographed at Woking on 24th August 1968. (Terry Gough)

116

LUGGAGE VANS

Detail from SECR luggage van number DS251 photographed at Woking on 24th August 1968. (Terry Gough)

LBSCR perishable and luggage van

Built by or for	LBSCR
SR diagram number	975
Description	13-ton perishable and luggage van (commonly known as a milk van)
Quantity built	69
Date	1908
Quantity at Nationalisation	2, both Departmental
Underframe material	timber
Wheelbase	9' 9" + 9' 9"
Body length	30' 0"
Overall length	32' 11"
Body width	8' 0"
Height above rails	11' 9½"
SR running numbers	2094 – 2156, 2175 – 2180
Departmental numbers (examples)	DS986(s) ex 2145, DS1525(s) ex 2178
Internal user numbers	none
Example extant	LBSCR 270 (SR 2178)
Location	BluebellR

Centre wheel springs are 8' between shackles and outer springs are 7'.

LBSCR perishable and luggage van number 270 photographed at Horsted Keynes on 25th May 1966. (Terry Gough)

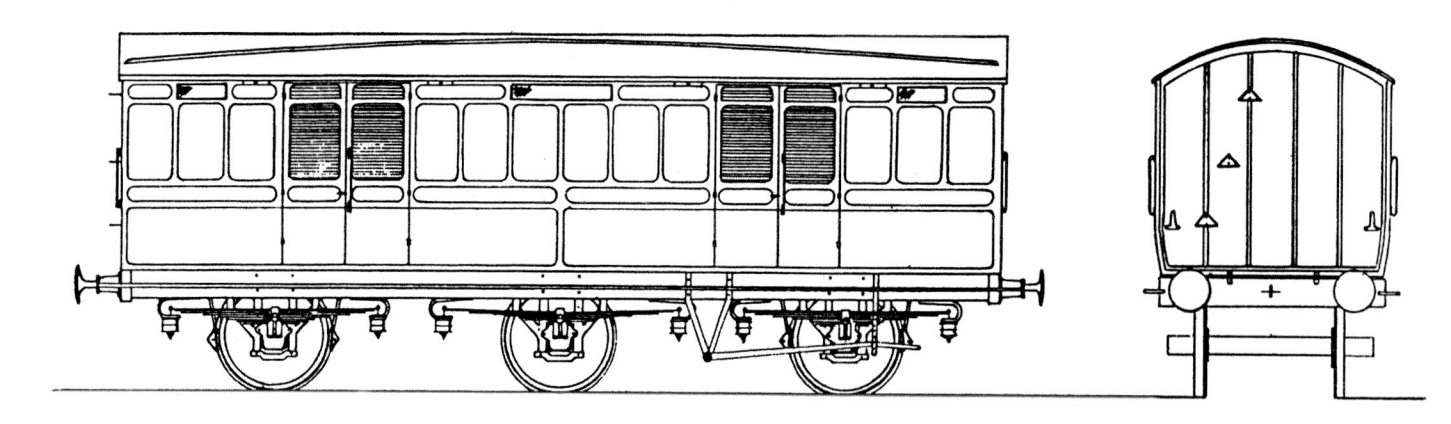

A PICTORIAL GUIDE TO SOUTHERN WAGONS AND VANS

LBSCR perishable and luggage van (diagram 975). (Gerry Bixley)

Above: LBSCR perishable and luggage van number DS1525 photographed at Lancing post-1948. (John Smith)

Left: Detail from LBSCR perishable and luggage van number 270 photographed at Horsted Keynes in October 1968. (Terry Gough)

LUGGAGE VANS

SR corridor luggage vans

Built by or for	SR	SR	SR
SR diagram number	3098	3099	3100
Description	25/26-ton bogie corridor luggage vans (SR GBL; BR COR PMV)		
Quantity built	33	37	50
Date	1930/1	1931	1930
Quantity at Nationalisation	all	all	all
Underframe material	steel	steel	steel
Bogie centres	34' 3"	36' 3"	36' 3"
Wheelbase	8' 0"	8' 0"	8' 0"
Body length	51' 3"	53' 3"	51' 3"
Overall length	54' 11"	56' 11"	54' 11"
Body width	7' 11"	7' 11"	7' 11"
Height above rails	12' 0"	12' 0"	12' 0"
SR running numbers (examples)	2331–2354, 2482–2490	2355–2370, 2461–2481	2281–2330
Departmental numbers (examples)	DS70083 ex 2332	DS70141 ex 2462	DS70036 ex 2286
Internal user numbers (examples)	081140 ex 2352	081615 ex 2476	081616 ex 2290
Examples extant	2339	2462	2464
Location	RotherR	BluebellR	See note below

Vehicles to all three diagrams consisted of new bodies on modified LSWR underframes and bogies that were surplus to requirements. No 2464 was used in the funeral train of Sir Winston Churchill and was subsequently exported to the USA. It was located on a golf course in south east Los Angeles until August 2007, when it began its journey back to the UK. Once restored it will be based on the Swanage Railway.

Three views of SR corridor luggage van number DS70083 photographed at Wimbledon in August 1968.
(Terry Gough)

A PICTORIAL GUIDE TO SOUTHERN WAGONS AND VANS

SR corridor luggage van (diagram 3098). (Terry Gough)

Model of an SR corridor luggage van (diagram 3099). (Terry Gough)

SR corridor luggage van number 081616 photographed at Feltham in August 1968. The gangway was boarded up when the van was transferred to internal use. (Terry Gough)

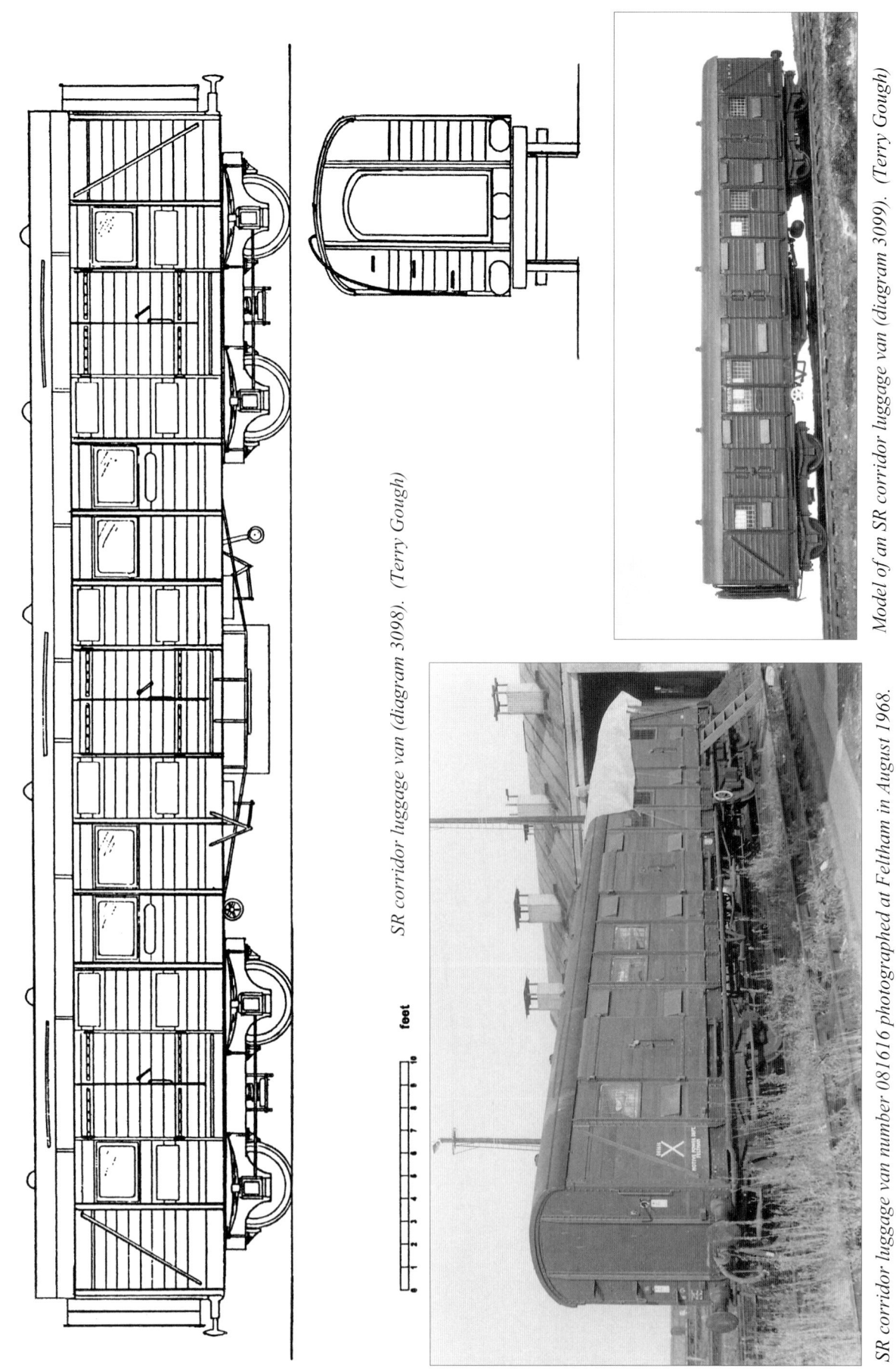

LUGGAGE VANS

SR corridor luggage van number 2464 photographed in Los Angeles on 22nd March 2006. (Terry Gough)

SR/BR luggage van

Built by or for	SR/BR
SR diagram number	3103
Description	12/13-ton luggage van (SR PLV; BR PMV)
Approximate quantity built	900
Date	1934 – 1951
Quantity at Nationalisation	all
Underframe material	steel
Wheelbase	21'0"
Body length	32' 0"
Overall length	35' 8"
Body width	7' 10"
Height above rails	12' 0"
SR running numbers (examples)	1054 – 1358 (wide planking), 1359 – 1398 (wide/narrow planking), 1561 – 1671 (plywood sheet), 1046 – 1052 IOW ex 1134, 1283, 1720, 1335, 1321, 1384, 1692
Departmental numbers (examples)	DS8 ex 1168, DS36 ex 2181, DS70314 ex 1150, ADB977182 ex 1507
Internal user numbers (examples)	082200 ex 1061, 083146 ex 1148, 083663 ex 2181, 082803 ex 1049 IOW
Examples extant and locations	1145 (KESR), 1174 (SevernR), 1184 (BluebellR), 1240 (SpaR), 1396 (ESomR), 1855 (BodminR), 2105 (ColneR), 2142 (BidefordC), DS8 (GwiliR), DS36 (ChasewaterR)

The main differences between these vans and their SECR forerunners are that ventilators are fitted to the body sides, which also have chalk "slates". From 1939 body sides were constructed of alternate pairs of wide (nominal 6½") and narrow (nominal 3½") planks. Prior to this all planking was 6½". In 1950 further changes were made and body sides (but not the doors) were constructed of plywood sheeting. The vans are still common, both on the National Network as Departmental and Internal User vehicles, and on heritage railways.

See SECR diagram 960 on page 116 for a drawing.

SR/BR luggage van number S1049 IOW photographed at Brading in August 1966. (Terry Gough)

SR/BR luggage van number S1883S photographed at Basingstoke in June 1965. (Terry Gough)

SR/BR luggage van number S1646S photographed at Clapham Junction on 31st August 1968. (Terry Gough)

LUGGAGE VANS

Above: Detail from SR/BR luggage van number S1646S photographed at Clapham Junction on 31st August 1968. (Terry Gough)

Right: End detail of 12/13-ton luggage van number 2142 photographed at Bideford on 18th September 2005. (Terry Gough)

Left: Model of an SR/BR luggage van (diagram 3103). (Terry Gough)

SR luggage van

Built by or for	SR
SR diagram number	3105
Description	10-ton luggage van (SR PLV; BR PMV)
Quantity built	10
Date	1943/44
Quantity at Nationalisation	all
Underframe material	steel
Wheelbase	22' 0"
Body length	32' 2½"
Length over headstocks	33' 0"
Overall length	36' 5"
Body width	8' 2½"
Height above rails	12' 5"
SR running numbers	1401 – 1410
Departmental numbers	none
Internal user numbers	082186 ex 1401, 082145 ex 1405
Examples extant	none

These most unusual vans had reinforced plastic bodies, which were a little shorter than the underframe, as clearly seen on the photographs on page 124. The photographs also reveal deterioration of the body, as evidenced by the blotchy effect. They were fitted with 3' 1½" diameter 3-hole disc wheels, rather than 3' 7" wheels normally used on passenger vans.

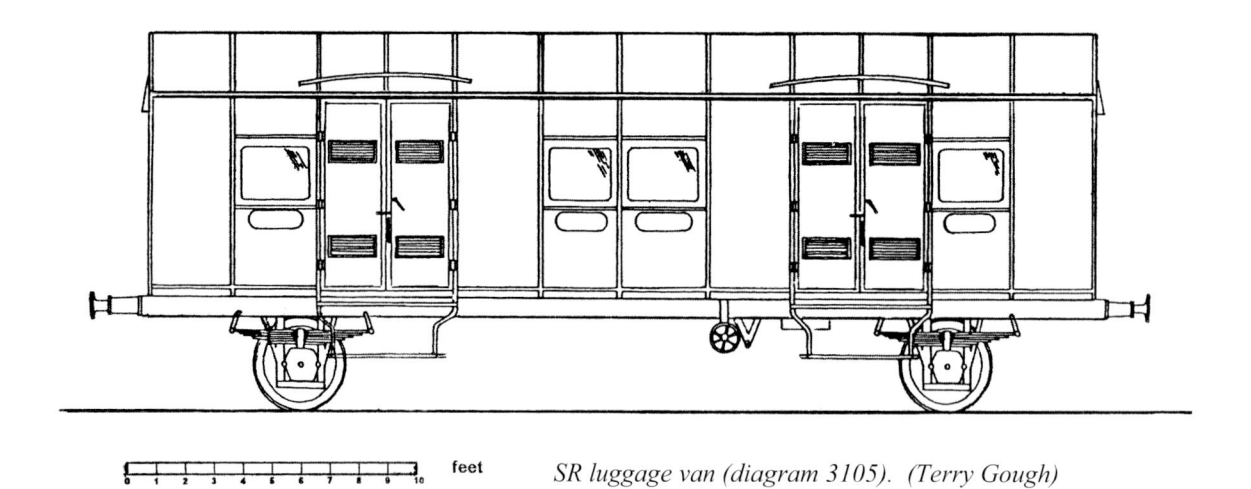

A PICTORIAL GUIDE TO SOUTHERN WAGONS AND VANS

SR luggage van (diagram 3105). (Terry Gough)

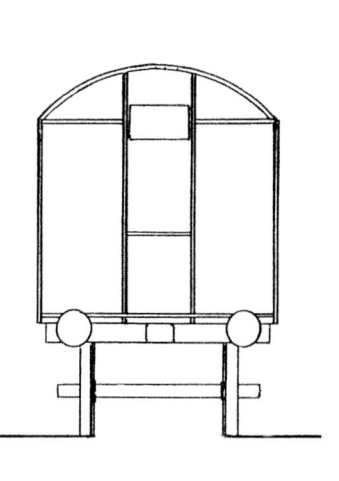

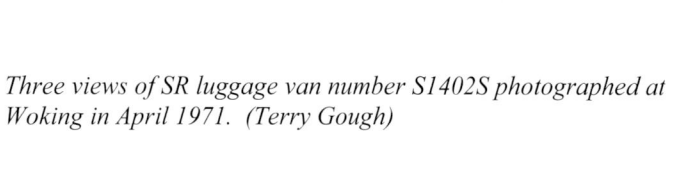

Three views of SR luggage van number S1402S photographed at Woking in April 1971. (Terry Gough)

124

COVERED CARRIAGE TRUCKS

Covered Carriage Trucks

SECR covered carriage truck

Built by or for	SECR
SR diagram number	1156
Description	13-ton covered carriage truck
Quantity built	20
Date	1905
Approximate quantity at Nationalisation	20, all Departmental
Underframe material	timber
Wheelbase	9' 9" + 9' 9"
Body length	32' 0"
Overall length	35' 10"
Body width	8' 0"
Height above rails	12' 4"
SR running numbers	4656 – 4675
Departmental numbers (examples)	DS1160(s) ex 4657, 916s ex 4664, DS1342(s) ex 4669, DS1450(s) ex 4670
Internal user numbers	none
Example extant	DS1450
Location	Sellinge

These vans were originally panelled, but several were sheeted over in later years. Doors were fitted at both ends.

Details from SECR covered carriage truck number DS1450 photographed at Wimbledon in August 1968. (Terry Gough)

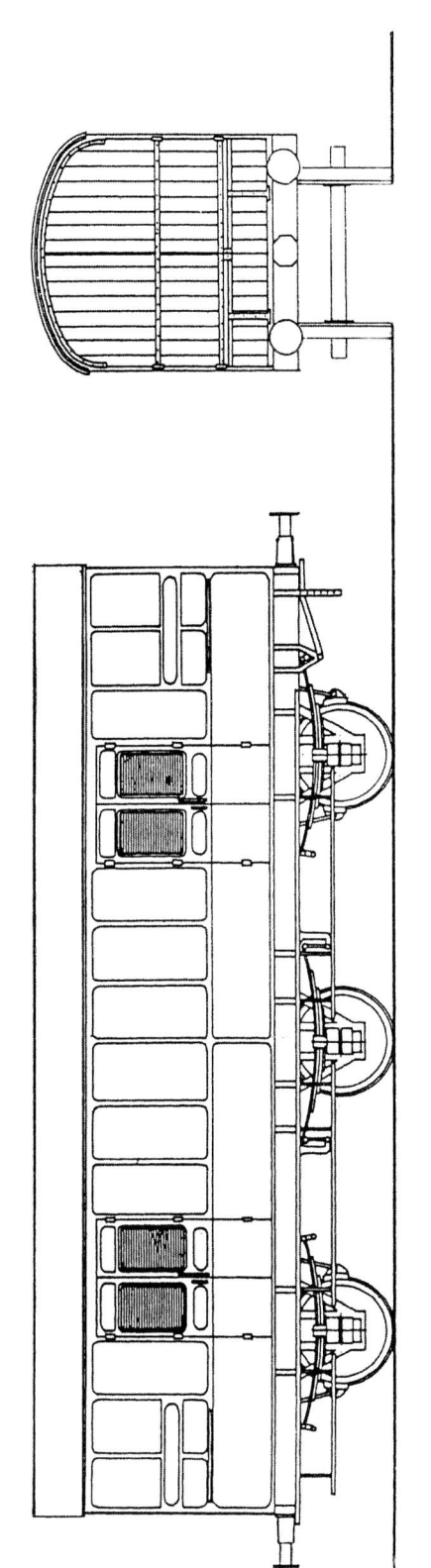

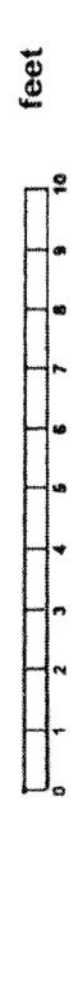

A PICTORIAL GUIDE TO SOUTHERN WAGONS AND VANS

Detail from SECR covered carriage truck number DS1450 photographed at Wimbledon in August 1968. (Terry Gough)

SECR covered carriage truck (diagram 1156). (Terry Gough)

SECR covered carriage truck number DS1450 photographed at Micheldever in October 1968. (Terry Gough)

COVERED CARRIAGE TRUCKS

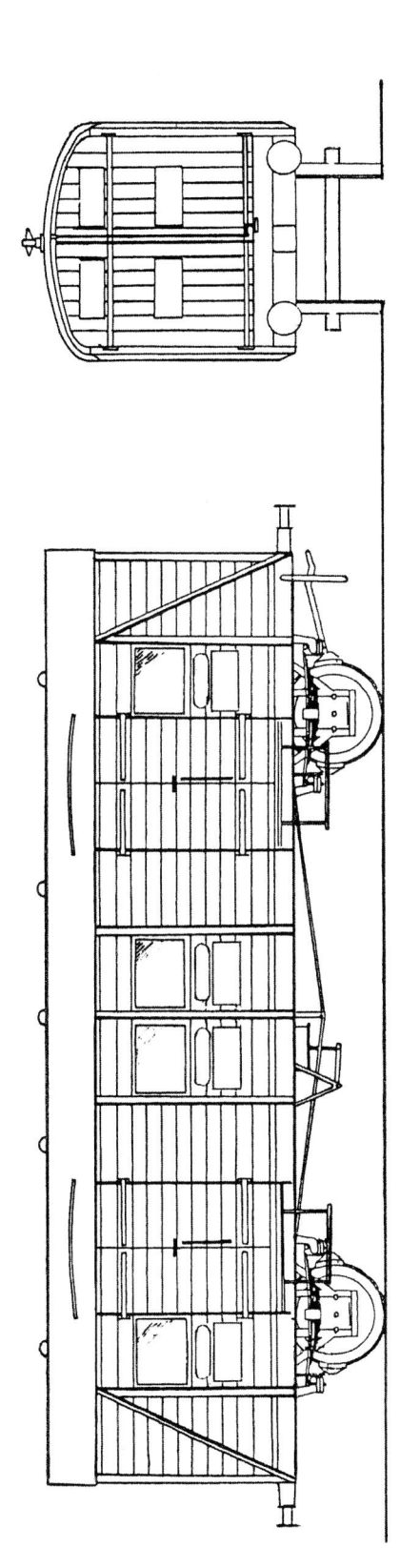

SR/BR covered carriage truck/general utility van (diagram 3101). (Terry Gough)

SR/BR covered carriage truck/general utility van number S1765S photographed at Wimbledon on 31st August 1968. (Terry Gough)

SR/BR covered carriage truck/general utility van number S1411S photographed at Barry on 25th August 1981. (Terry Gough)

A PICTORIAL GUIDE TO SOUTHERN WAGONS AND VANS

SR/BR covered carriage truck/general utility van

Built by or for	SR/BR
SR diagram number	3101
Description	13/14-ton covered carriage truck/general utility van (SR Van U; BR CCT)
Approximate quantity built	400
Date	1928 – 1955
Quantity at Nationalisation	all
Underframe material	steel
Wheelbase	21' 0"
Body length	32' 4", some 32' 6"
Overall length	35' 10"
Body width	7' 10"
Height above rails	12' 0"
SR running numbers (examples)	1731 – 1780 (wide/narrow planking), 1977 – 1991 (plywood), 2491 – 2500 (equal width planking)
Departmental numbers (examples)	ADB977039 ex 1989, DS70239 ex 2373, DS70324 ex 2439, DS70264 ex 2497
Internal user numbers (examples)	081646 ex 2257, 082949 ex 2400
Examples extant	1745 2239 2276 DS70239
Location	KESR SpaR BluebellR WightR

Three different types of bodywork, all under the same overall dimensions. For details see under diagram 3103 (page 121).

SR/BR covered carriage truck/general utility van number DS70264 photographed at Woking in October 1968. This view shows a much modified van, with several extra windows. (Terry Gough)

Above: SR/BR covered carriage truck/general utility van number S2379S photographed at Stewarts Lane on 31ˢᵗ August 1968. (Terry Gough)

Right: Model of an SR/BR covered carriage truck/general utility van (diagram 3101). (Terry Gough)

COVERED CARRIAGE TRUCKS

SR/BR covered carriage truck/scenery vans

Built by or for	SR	SR/BR
SR diagram number	3181	3182
Description	22-ton bogie scenery van (SR CCT; BR CCT or GUV)	24/25-ton bogie scenery van
Quantity built	10	20
Date	1928/29	1938/49
Quantity at Nationalisation	all	all
Underframe material	steel	steel
Bogie centres	33' 0"	34' 10"
Wheelbase	8' 0"	8' 0"
Body length	50' 0"	50' 0"
Overall length	53' 7½"	53' 8½"
Body width	7' 10"	7' 10"
Height above rails	12' 8"	12' 8"
SR running numbers	4577 – 4586	4587 – 4606
Departmental numbers (examples)		ADB975889 ex 4602, TDB975967 ex 4605
Internal user numbers (examples)		083361 ex 4588, 083379 ex 4598
Examples extant		4590 4594 4595
Location		GlosR SwanageR EKR
Examples extant		4601 4605 4606
Location		BluebellR WightR GwiliR

Vans to diagram 3181 are on LBSCR underframes with LSWR bogies. Vans to diagram 3182 are on new underframes with standard SR bogies, as illustrated under diagram 3191 (page 147).

SR/BR scenery van number S4594S photographed at Woking in August 1968. (Terry Gough)

A PICTORIAL GUIDE TO SOUTHERN WAGONS AND VANS

SR/BR scenery van (diagram 3182). (Terry Gough)

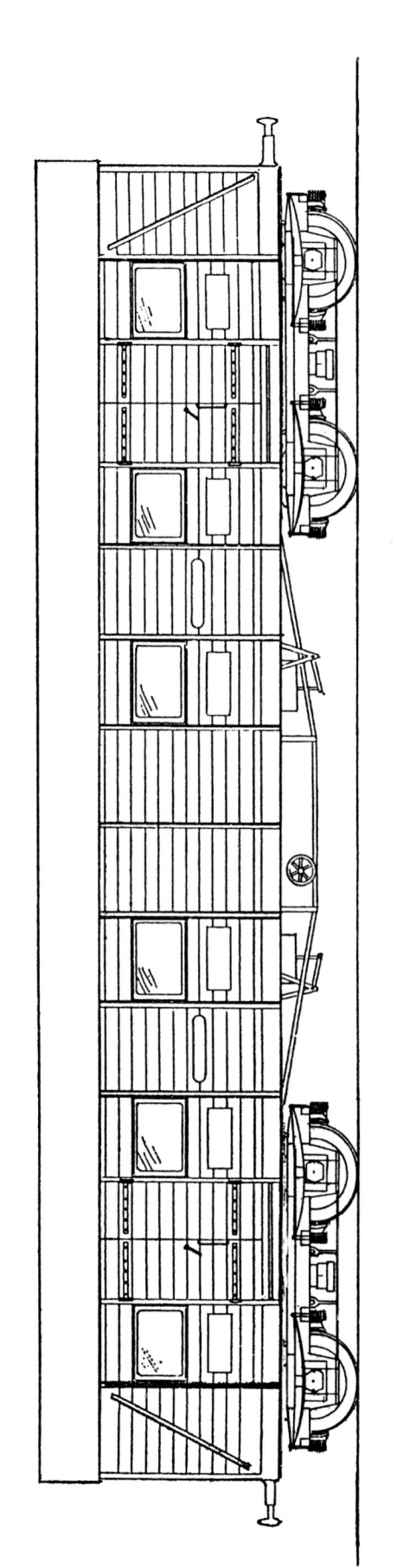

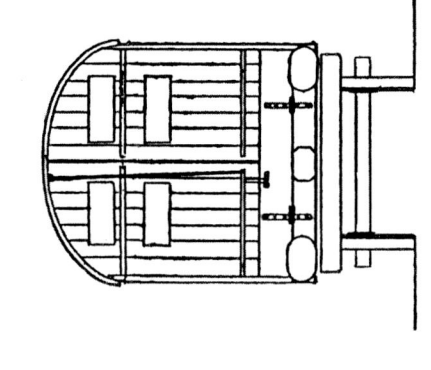

End detail of an unrecorded scenery van photographed at Wolverhampton in August 1966. (Terry Gough)

SR/BR scenery van number S4604S photographed at Woking in October 1964. (Terry Gough)

130

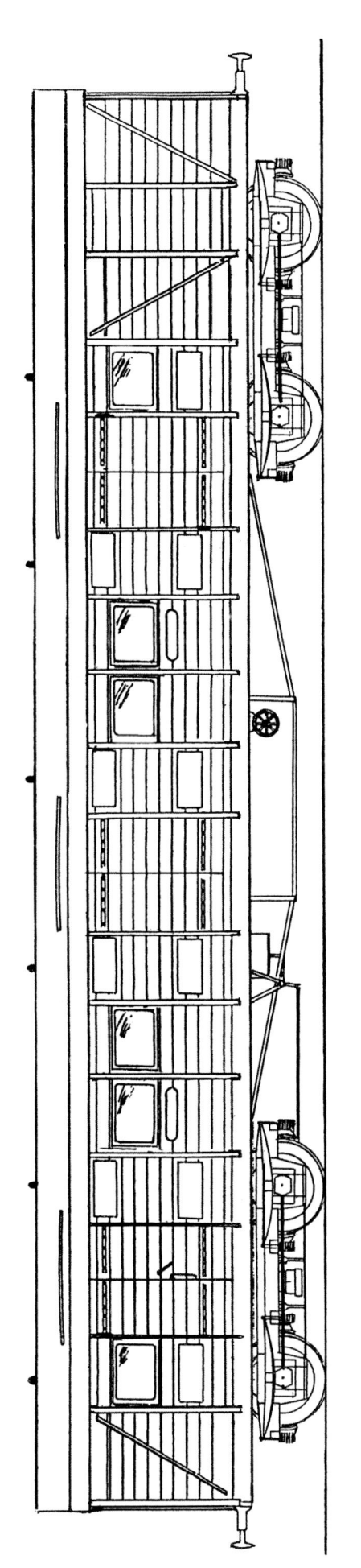

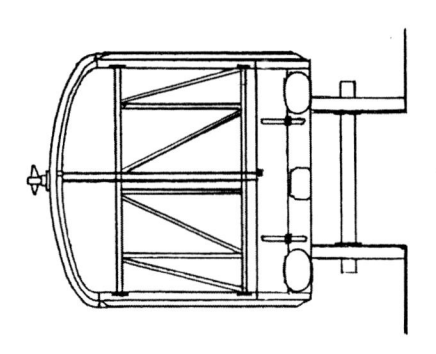

SR/BR covered motor car van (diagram 3183). (Terry Gough)

SR/BR covered motor car van

Built by or for	SR/BR
SR diagram number	3183
Description	26-ton bogie covered motor car van (BR CCT or MCV)
Quantity built	1
Date	1960
Underframe material	steel
Bogie centres	40' 0"
Wheelbase	8' 0"
Body length	58' 0"
Overall length	61' 7"
Body width	7' 11"
Height above rails	12' 5"
SR running numbers	4501
Departmental numbers	none
Internal user numbers	none
Examples extant	none

This unique vehicle was built from bogie luggage van number 2292 (of diagram 3100), which was extended at one end and mounted on an SR coach underframe. It was fitted with double doors both ends, and two pairs of the double doors on each side were sealed.

SR/BR covered motor car van number S4501S photographed at Eastleigh in 23rd December 1965. (Terry Gough)

Milk Tankers

There was a daily milk train between the West of England and London for decades, and these are the return empties on the afternoon of 31st May 1963. They are seen in Deepcut Cutting, between Brookwood and Farnborough behind Class N No 31810. (Terry Gough)

Much further west, at Seaton Junction, Class M7 No 30048 shunts some milk tankers into the depot in between running the push pull service to Seaton on 7th March 1966. (Terry Gough)

SR mobile tank carriage truck

Built by or for	SR
SR diagram number	3154
Description	11-ton mobile tank carriage truck
Quantity built	7
Date built	1932/33
Quantity at Nationalisation	all
Underframe material	steel
Wheelbase	6' 6"+6' 6"
Wheel diameter	3' 1½"
Length over headstocks	20' 6"
Overall length	23' 11"
Width over runway plates	8' 6"
SR running numbers	4414 – 4418, 4425, 4426
Departmental numbers	none
Internal user numbers	none
Example extant	W3030 (GWR diagram No 049, which is similar, but 4' longer)
Location	DidcotC

These trucks were used with road trailers manufactured by Dyson. The trailers were designed in 1931 in conjunction with the SR and GWR. Each trailer consisted of a 2,000 gallon steel tank attached by short chassis members to two axles fitted with large wheels with pneumatic tyres. Some trailers had three axles. Draw gear was at one end, steering at both ends. There were other trailers designed by Dyson that had draw gear at both ends. The photograph of the GWR truck has been included because it is the closest extant vehicle to the SR truck and is complete with a road trailer.

The underframe to diagram 3154 is the same as that to diagram 3155 (page 136).

GWR mobile tank carriage truck number W3030 and road trailer photographed at Didcot on 14th July 2005. (Terry Gough)

MILK TANKERS

SR fixed milk tank wagon

Built by or for	SR	SR
SR diagram number	3152	3159
Description	14-ton fixed milk tank wagon	
Quantity built	6	6
Date built/rebuilt	1931	1937/38
Quantity at Nationalisation	none	all
Underframe material	steel	steel
Wheelbase	12' 0"	6' 6"+6' 6"
Wheel diameter	3' 1½"	3' 1½"
Tank length	18' 5"	18' 5"
Tank diameter	6' 5½"	6' 5½"
Length over headstocks	21' 6"	20' 6"
Width over headstocks	6' 11"	6' 10½"
Overall length	24' 11"	23' 11"
Overall height above rails	11' 4½"	11' 4½"
SR running numbers	4404 – 4409	4404 – 4409
Departmental numbers	none	none known
Internal user numbers	none	none known
Example extant	none	4409
Location		DidcotC

The 4-wheeled wagons of diagram 3152 were withdrawn 1937/38 and the tanks fitted to new 6-wheeled chassis (see diagram 3155 on page 136). These rebuilt wagons were given diagram 3159.

SR fixed milk tank wagon number 4409 photographed at Didcot on 14th July 2005. (Terry Gough)

A PICTORIAL GUIDE TO SOUTHERN WAGONS AND VANS

SR fixed milk tank wagon

Built by or for	SR	SR	SR
SR diagram number	3155	3156	3157
Description	14-ton fixed milk tank wagons		
Quantity built	6	2	16
Date	1932	1933	1933-1945
Quantity at Nationalisation	all	both	all
Underframe material	steel	steel	steel
Wheelbase	6' 6"+6' 6"	6' 6"+6' 6"	6' 6"+6' 6"
Wheel diameter	3' 1½"	3' 1½"	3' 1½"
Tank length	18' 5"	18' 5"	18' 5"
Tank diameter	6' 5½"	6' 5½"	6' 5½"
Length over headstocks	20' 6"	20' 6"	20' 6"
Width over headstocks	6' 10½"	6' 10½"	6' 10½"
Overall length	23' 11"	23' 11"	23' 11"
Overall height above rails	11' 4½"	11' 5"	11' 4½"
SR running numbers	4419 – 4424	4427/28	4429 – 4432, 4455 – 4466
Departmental number (example)			DS4459
Internal user numbers	none	none	none
Examples extant	none	none	4430
Location			BluebellR

DS4459 was marked "NOT TO BE USED FOR MILK". The two vehicles to diagram 3156 had canopies over the top part of the tanks.

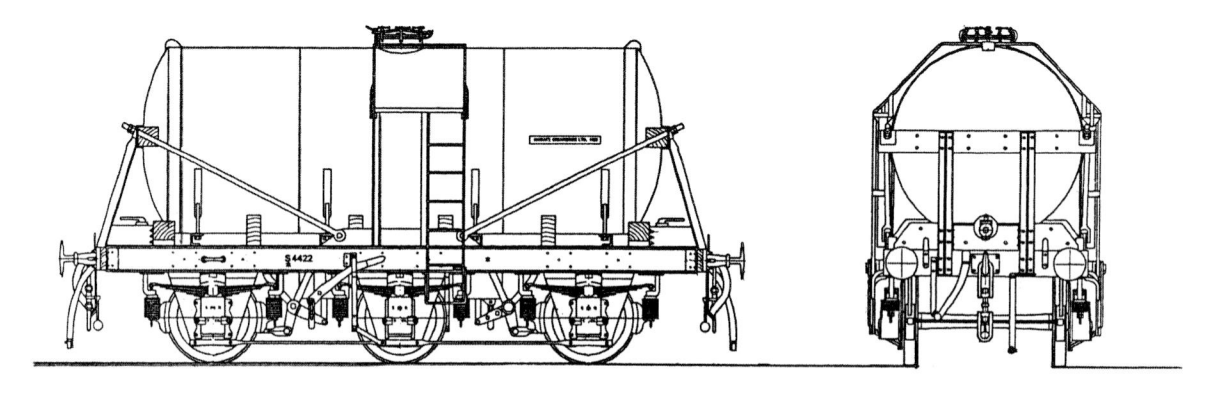

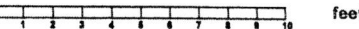

SR fixed milk tank wagon (diagram 3155). (Glen Woods)

SR fixed milk tank wagon number S4423 photographed at Totnes in September 1971. (Terry Gough)

MILK TANKERS

SR fixed milk tank wagon number S4429 photographed at Totnes in January 1967. (Terry Gough)

SR fixed milk tank wagon number DS4459 photographed in April 1973. (Terry Gough)

Models of SR fixed milk tank wagons to diagrams 3156 and 3157. (Terry Gough)

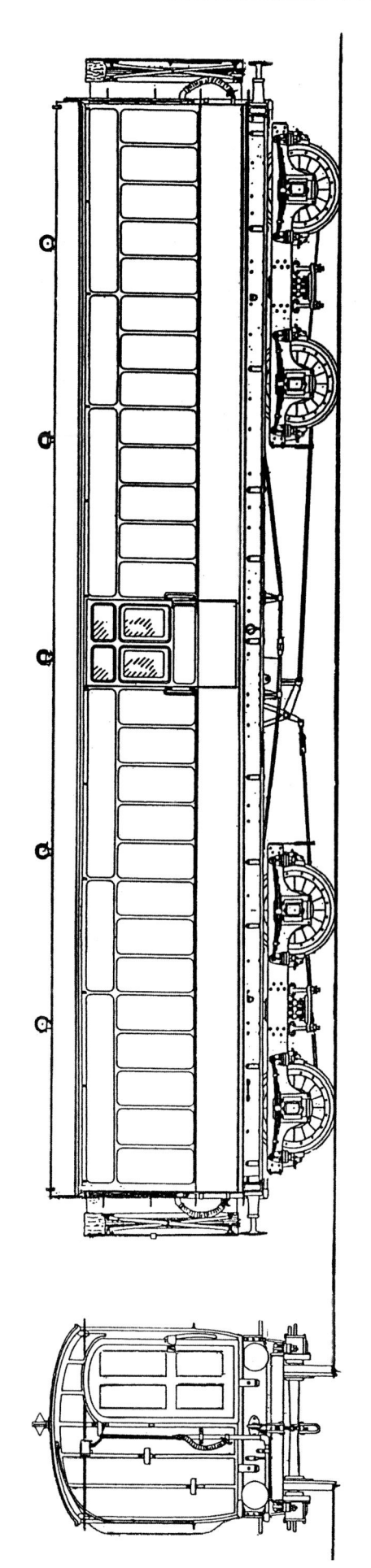

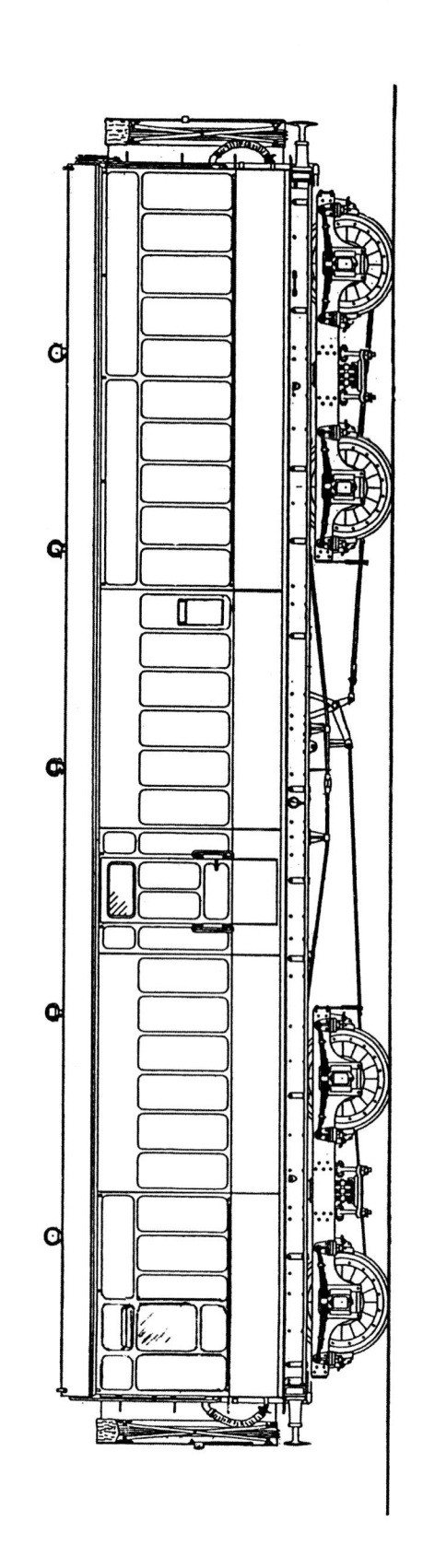

LSWR Post Office van (sorting) (diagram 1184A). Side A: top, side B: bottom. (Gordon Weddell)

Post Office Vans

LSWR Post Office van (sorting)

Built by or for	LSWR
SR Diagram number	1184A
Description	bogie Post Office van (sorting)
Quantity built	2
Date	1898, 1900
Quantity at Nationalisation	1
Underframe material	steel
Bogie centres	29' 3"
Wheelbase	8' 0"
Body length	44' 0"
Overall length	47' 11"
Body width	8' 1", 8' 6" over bulge
Height above rails	12' 2"
SR running numbers	4906, 4911
Departmental number	1448s ex 4911
Internal user numbers	none
Examples extant	none

These vans had offset gangways. The gangway side has been designated Side A and the other is Side B.
For an illustration of the bogies see page 100.
Battery boxes were removed from 4911 once it entered Departmental service.

Side A of LSWR Post Office sorting van number 1448s photographed at Wimbledon on 8th April 1958. (David Wigley)

Above: Side B of LSWR Post Office sorting van number 1448s photographed at Wimbledon in the 1950s. (John Smith)

Right: Detail of side A of LSWR Post Office sorting van number 1448s photographed at Wimbledon in the 1950s. (John Smith)

SECR Post Office vans (sorting)

Built by or for	SECR
SR Diagram number	1205, 1206
Description	5-ton bogie Post Office vans (sorting)
Quantity built	3
Date	1904
Quantity at Nationalisation	all
Underframe material	timber/steel
Bogie centres	33' 6"
Wheelbase	8' 0"
Body length	50' 1"
Overall length	53' 10"
Body width	8' 1"
Height above rails	11' 8½" + lights = 12' 2"
SR running numbers	4951 diagram 1205, 4952/53 diagram 1206
Departmental numbers (example)	1889s ex 4951 temporarily
Internal user numbers (example)	081039 ex 4951
Examples extant	none

All the vans had offset gangways. The gangway side has been designated side A and the other is side B. No 4951 (diagram 1205) had a gangway only at one end (right hand end of side A on drawing). Side B of the vans to both diagrams had a single centre hinged door (see page 142). Only 4952 and 4953 (both diagram 1206) were originally fitted with net apparatus on side A, which was soon removed, although the recess was retained. Body panels were covered in steel sheet in later (probably BR) years, and the recess for the net apparatus removed (see photograph on page 141). No 4953 had a lavatory added in BR days. No 4952 was converted to a stowage van in 1951. It also had two pairs of hinged doors added on side B, most probably at the same time. Each van was fitted with eight roof lights, which were retained throughout their existence.

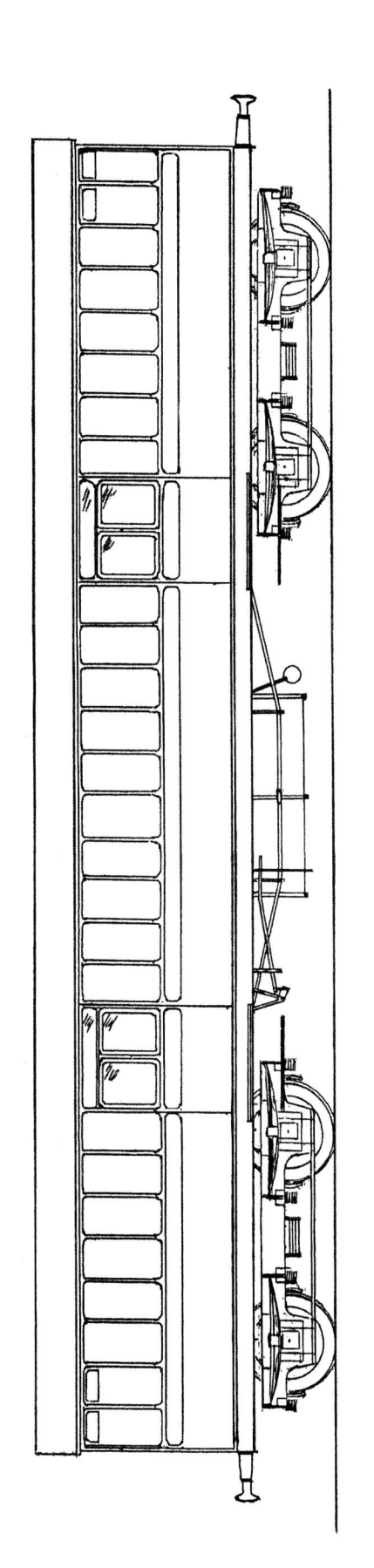

POST OFFICE VANS

Side A of SECR Post Office sorting van (diagram 1205). (Terry Gough)

Above: Van ends (diagrams 961, 1205, 1206, 1207, and 1208. (Terry Gough)

Left: Side A of SECR Post Office sorting van number 081039 at Lancing, post 1959. (John Smith)

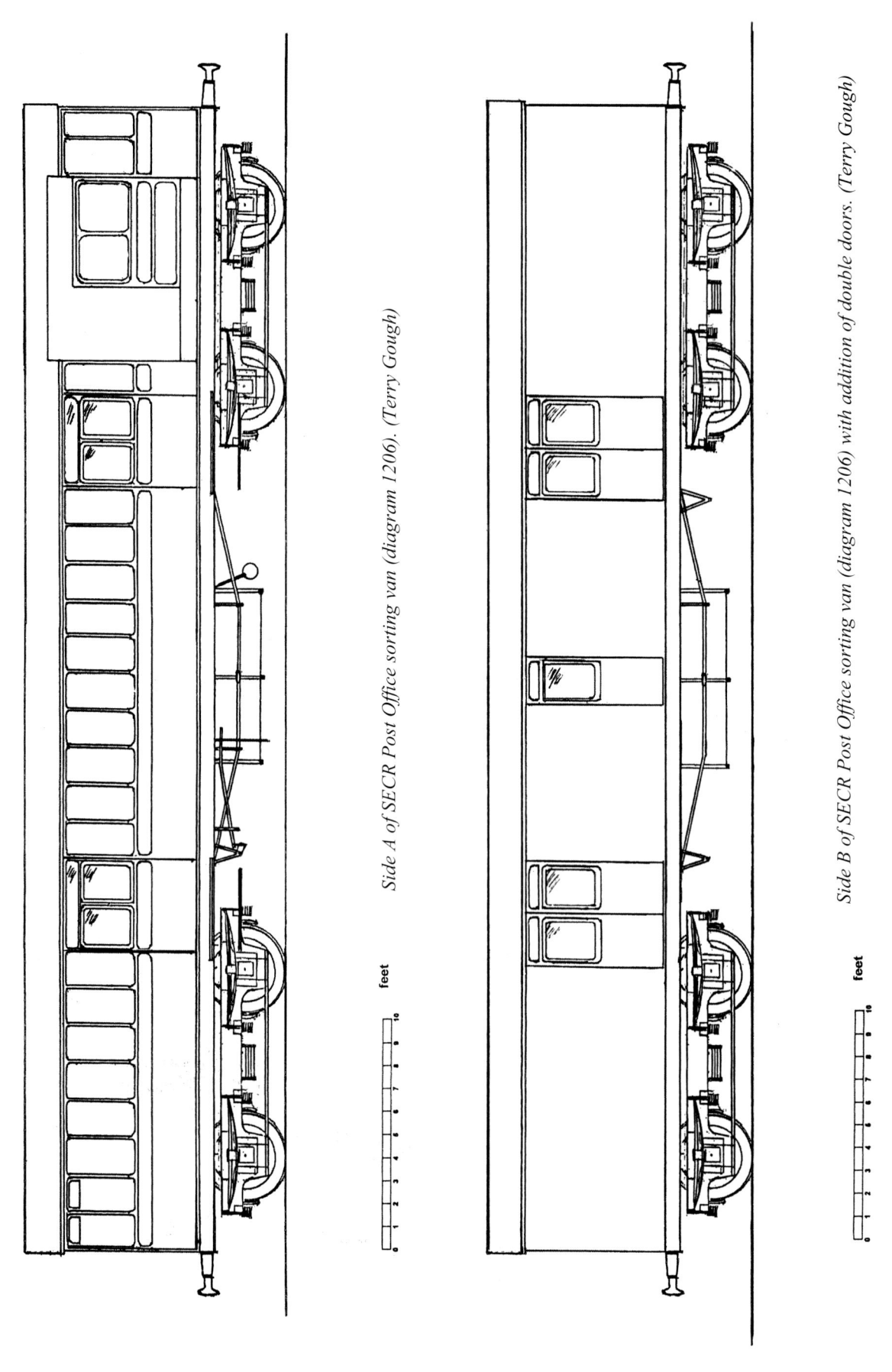

Side A of SECR Post Office sorting van (diagram 1206). (Terry Gough)

Side B of SECR Post Office sorting van (diagram 1206) with addition of double doors. (Terry Gough)

POST OFFICE VANS

Side B of SECR Post Office sorting van number S4952 photographed at Lancing on 5th September 1951. (J.H. Aston)

SECR luggage van, Post Office van (stowage)

Built by or for	SECR
SR Diagram number	961, 1207, 1208
Description	9-ton bogie luggage van, Post Office van (stowage)
Quantity built	5
Date	1907
Quantity at Nationalisation	all
Underframe material	steel
Bogie centres	33' 6"
Wheelbase	8' 0"
Body length	50' 1"
Overall length	53' 10"
Body width	8' 1"
Height above rails	11' 8½" + lights = 12' 2"
SR running numbers	2018 later 4954, 2019 later 4955 diagram 1207
	2020 later 4956 diagram 1208
	2021, 2022 diagram 961
Departmental numbers (examples)	DS221(s) ex 2021, DS188(s) ex 2022
Internal user number (example)	080539 ex 4956
Examples extant	none

The SR initially classified all the vehicles as luggage vans to diagram 961, but later reverted to the SECR description of stowage vans.

Gangways on all the vans were offset. See page 141 for the van ends. The two sides of all vans were similar, each with two recessed sliding doors. The drawing shows Side B for diagram 1207. For Side A diagram 1207, there is panelling instead of the lavatory window. Vans to diagrams 961 and 1208 were indistinguishable externally. They did not have lavatories and both sides of each van were fully panelled and identical.

A PICTORIAL GUIDE TO SOUTHERN WAGONS AND VANS

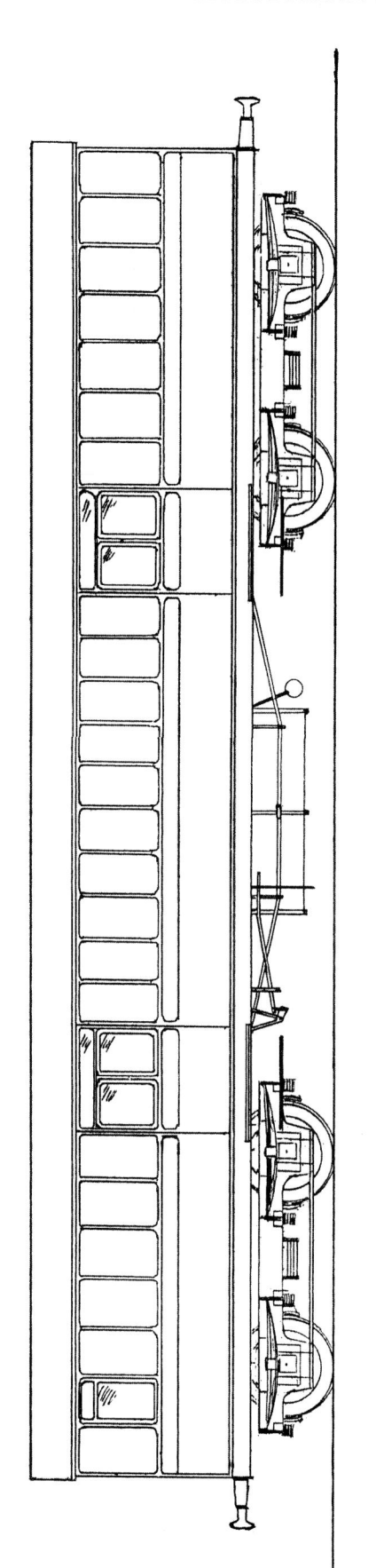

Side B of SECR Post Office stowage van (diagram 1207). (Terry Gough)

SECR Post Office stowage van number DS221. (John Smith)

SECR Post Office stowage van number S4954S. (John Smith)

POST OFFICE VANS

SR Post Office van (sorting)

Built by or for	SR	SR
SR Diagram number	3191	3192
Description	bogie Post Office van (sorting) (BR POS)	
Quantity built	1	3
Date	1936	1939
Quantity at Nationalisation	1	3
Underframe material	steel	steel
Bogie centres	40' 0"	40' 0"
Wheelbase	8' 0"	8' 0"
Body length	58' 0"	58' 0"
Overall length	61' 7"	61' 7"
Body width	9' 0"	9' 0"
Height above rails	12' 4"	12' 4"
SR running numbers	4919	4920 – 4922
Departmental numbers	none	none
Internal user numbers	none	none
Examples extant	none	4920 4922
Location		NeneR BluebellR

Side A is externally identical for both diagrams. There are internal differences between the vehicles to the two diagrams, which affect the position of the double door on side B. The vans to diagram 3192 were fitted with lavatories, the top of the tank protruding above the roof at this end. Toilet windows were later blocked out (see bottom photograph, this page). There is a raised roof section on both ends of the van to diagram 3191 and this addition was made in 1964 (see photograph on next page).

SR Post Office sorting van number S4920S photographed at Clapham Junction in May 1969. Above: Side A. Left: Side B. (Terry Gough)

A PICTORIAL GUIDE TO SOUTHERN WAGONS AND VANS

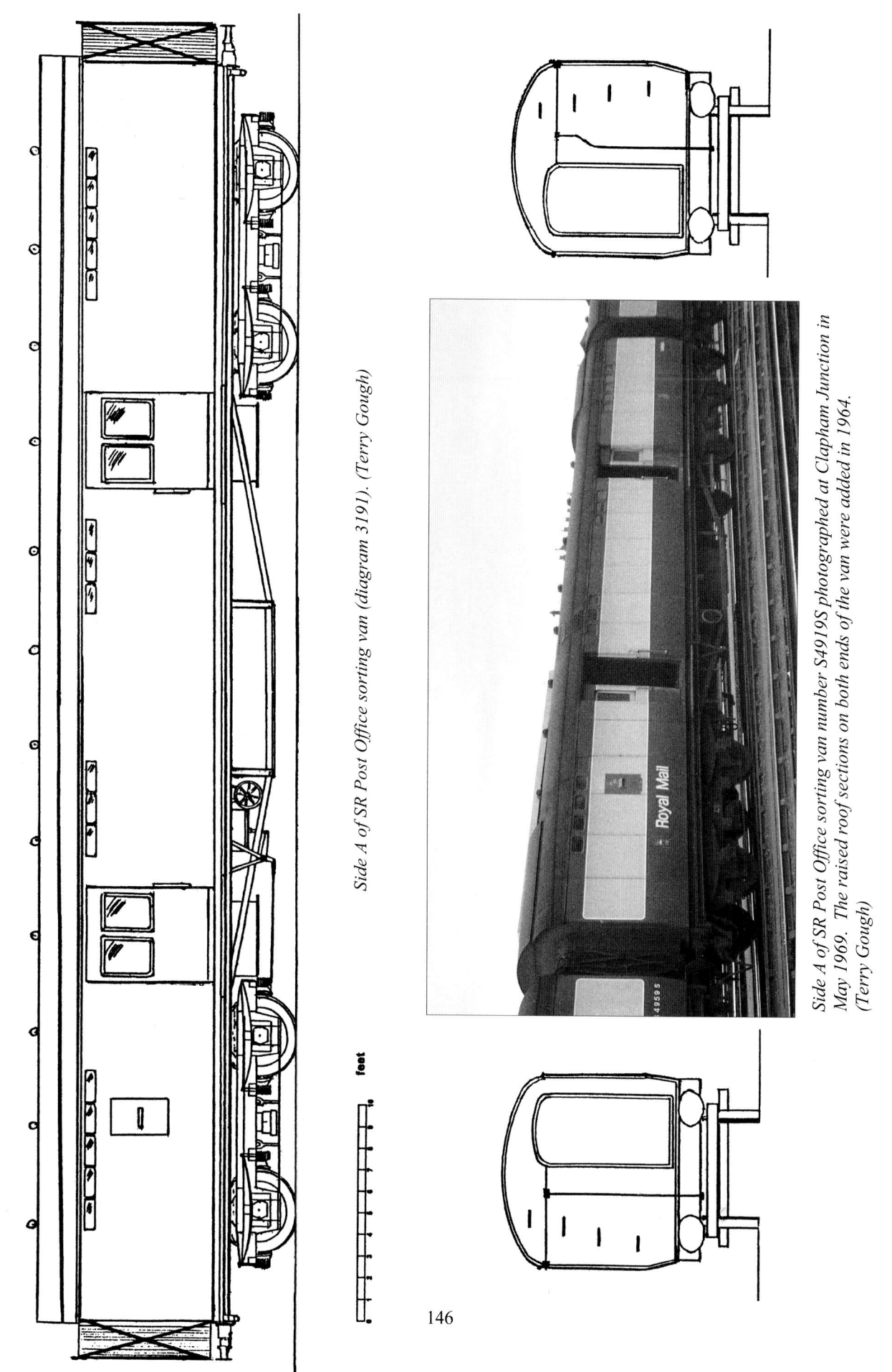

Side A of SR Post Office sorting van (diagram 3191). (Terry Gough)

Side A of SR Post Office sorting van number S4919S photographed at Clapham Junction in May 1969. The raised roof sections on both ends of the van were added in 1964. (Terry Gough)

146

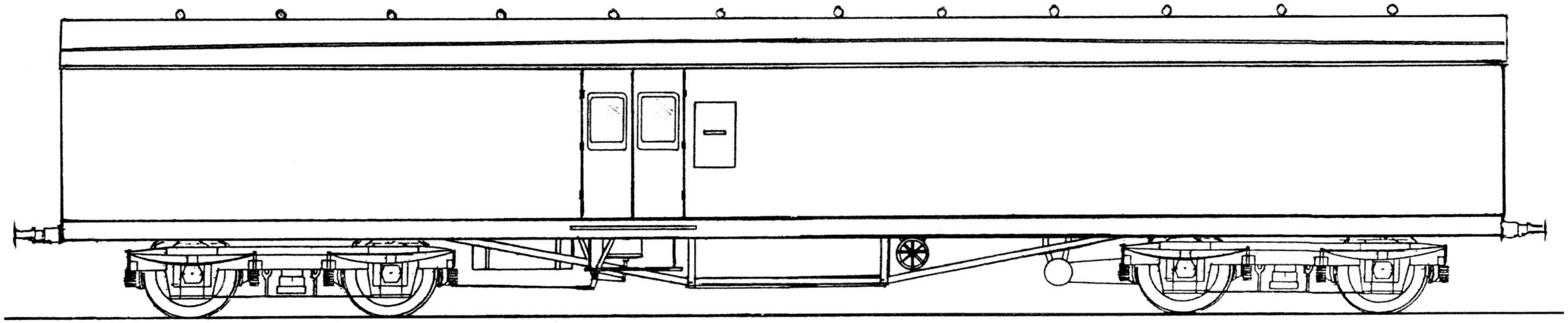

POST OFFICE VANS

Side B of SR Post Office sorting van (diagram 3191). (Terry Gough)

SR bogie photographed at Norden on 12th December 2005. (Terry Gough)

Side B of SR Post Office sorting van number S4919S photographed a Clapham Junction in May 1969. (Terry Gough)

147

Side A of SR Post Office sorting van (diagram 3192). (Terry Gough)

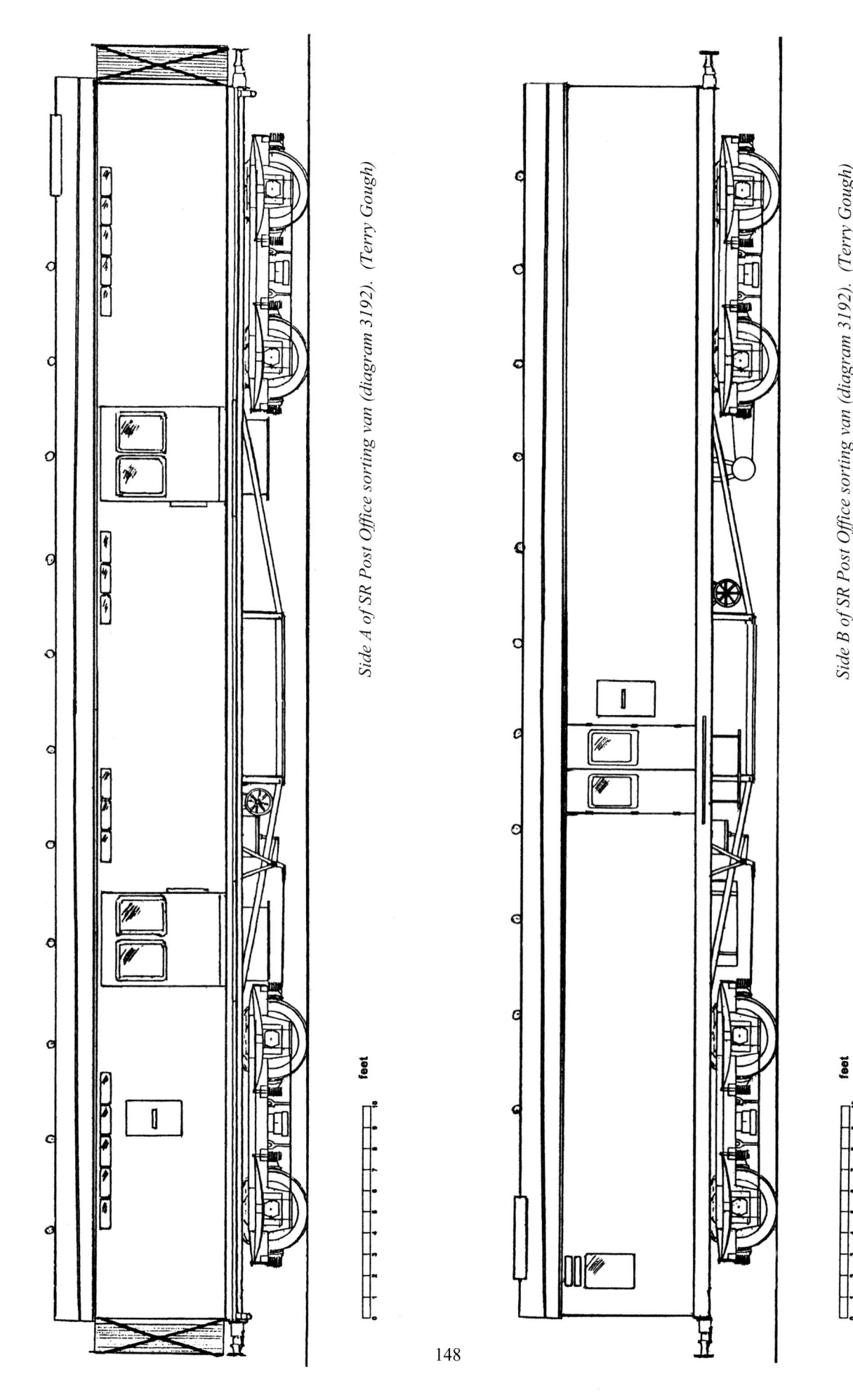

Side B of SR Post Office sorting van (diagram 3192). (Terry Gough)

POST OFFICE VANS

SR Post Office van (stowage)

Built by or for	SR
SR Diagram number	3196
Description	bogie Post Office van (stowage) (BR POT)
Quantity built	4
Date	1939
Quantity at Nationalisation	all
Underframe material	steel
Bogie centres	40' 0"
Wheelbase	8' 0"
Body length	58' 0"
Overall length	61' 7"
Body width	9' 0"
Height above rails	12' 4"
SR running numbers	4957 – 4960
Departmental numbers	none
Internal user numbers	none
Example extant	4958
Location	HantsR

All had offset gangways. Apart from an additional top light side A, there was no difference between the two sides. For bogies see under diagram 3191 on page 147.

Side A of SR Post Office stowage van number 4958 photographed at Ropley on 27th January 2006. (Terry Gough)

Side B of SR Post Office stowage van number S4959S photographed at Clapham Junction in May 1969. (Terry Gough)

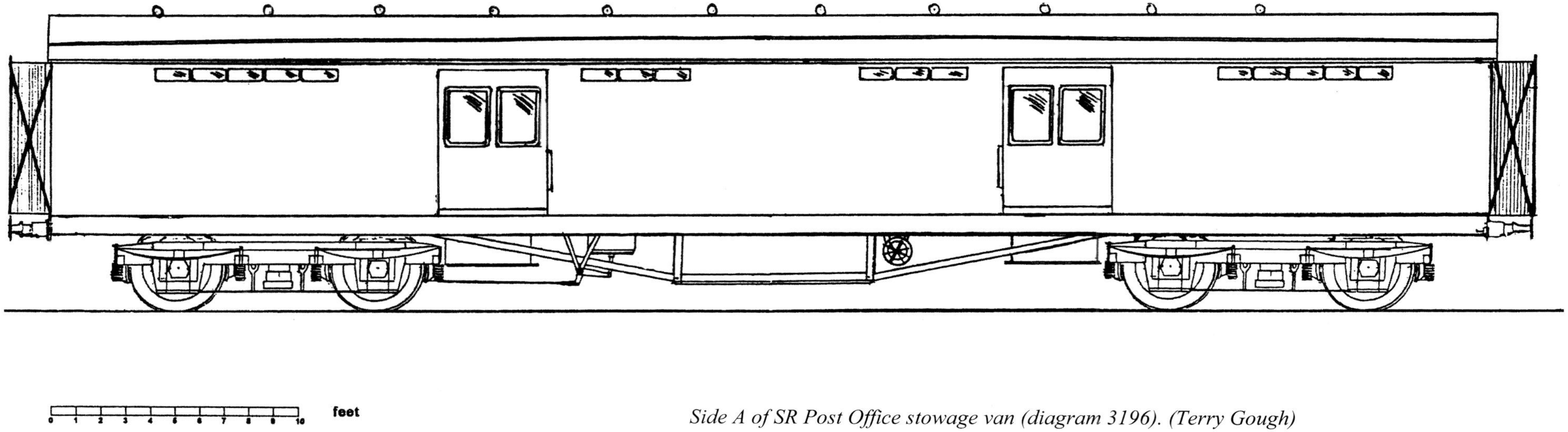

Side A of SR Post Office stowage van (diagram 3196). (Terry Gough)

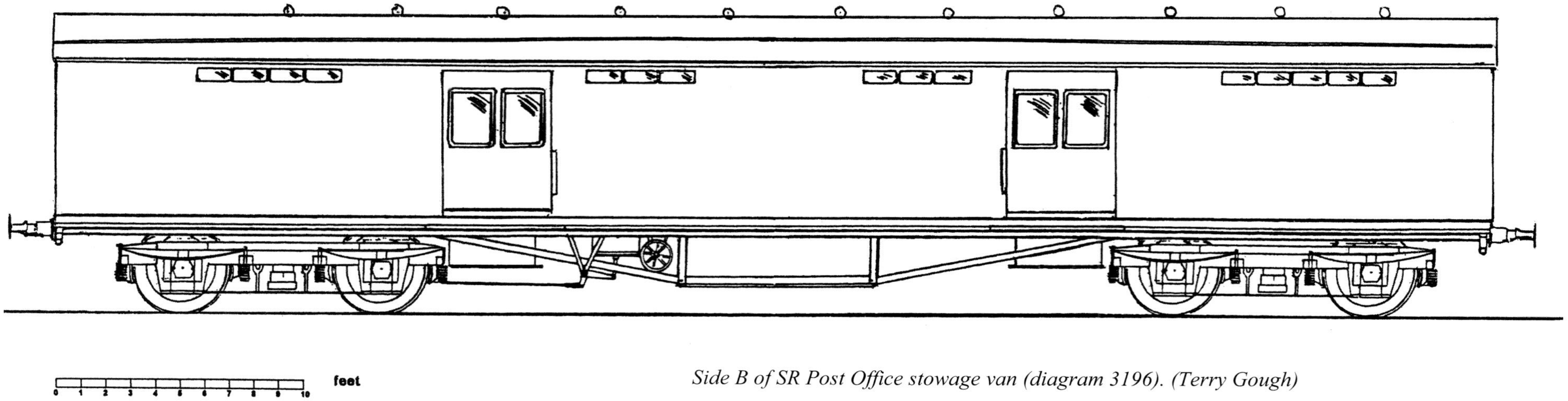

Side B of SR Post Office stowage van (diagram 3196). (Terry Gough)

INDEX

Index of Rolling Stock by SR and BR Diagram Number

Diagram No	Vehicle	Page
853	LSWR 6-wheeled guard's van	96, 97
863	LSWR bogie guard's van	99
870	LSWR bogie guard's van	97
884	SER/SECR 6-wheeled guard's van	101
885	SECR 6-wheeled guard's van	101
891	SECR/SR bogie guard's van	104
929	LSWR ventilated van	112
932	LSWR 6-wheeled ventilated van	111
940	LSWR bogie bullion van	114
960	SECR luggage van	116
961	SECR bogie luggage van	143
975	LBSCR 6-wheeled luggage van	117
1051	SECR special cattle van	30
1156	SECR 6-wheeled covered carriage truck	125
1184A	LSWR bogie Post Office van (sorting)	138
1205	SECR bogie Post Office van (sorting)	140
1206	SECR bogie Post Office van (sorting)	140
1207	SECR bogie Post Office van (stowage)	143
1208	SECR bogie Post Office van (stowage)	143
1352	SECR 4-plank dropside open goods wagon	2
1369	LBSCR 5-plank open goods wagon	3
1375	SR 5-plank open goods wagon	8
1379	SR 8-plank open goods wagon	5
1382, 1382A	SR container truck (short)	75
1383	SR container truck (long)	76
1386	SR 8-plank mineral wagon	6
1392	SR/BR 5-plank shock-absorbing open goods wagon	10
1399	SR container truck (short)	75
1400	SR 8-plank open goods wagon	7
1401	LSWR ventilated covered goods wagon	14
1402	LSWR ventilated covered goods wagon	14
1408	LSWR/SR covered goods wagon	15
1409	LSWR covered goods wagon	15
1410	LSWR covered goods wagon	12
1425	SECR covered goods wagon	18
1426	SECR/SR covered goods wagon	19
1428	SR covered goods wagon	20
1433	LBSCR covered goods wagon	16
1436	LBSCR covered goods wagon	16
1452	SR/BR covered goods wagon	23
1455	SR covered goods wagon	23
1457	see 1527 and 1528	31
1458	SR covered goods wagon	21
1478	SR banana van	25
1479	SR banana van	26
1501	LSWR cattle wagon	29
1502	LSWR cattle wagon	29
1515	see 1051	30
1527	LBSCR cattle wagon	31
1528	LBSCR large cattle wagon	31
1529	SR/BR large cattle wagon	35
1530	SR/BR large cattle wagon	35
1541	LSWR goods brake van	40
1541 rebuild	LSWR/SR goods brake van	42
1542	LSWR goods brake van	43
1543	LSWR goods brake van	45
1550	SR bogie goods brake van	59
1558	SECR 6-wheeled goods brake van	46
1559	SECR goods brake van	48
1560	SR goods brake van	48
1576	LBSCR/SR goods brake van	50
1578	SR goods brake van	52
1579	SR goods brake van	53

A PICTORIAL GUIDE TO SOUTHERN WAGONS AND VANS

Diagram No	Vehicle	Page
1580	LBSCR/SR bogie goods brake van	56
1581	SR goods brake van	57
1582	SR goods brake van	53
1597	LSWR/SR bogie bolster wagon	62
1598	SR bogie bolster wagon	65
1599	SR bogie bolster wagon	65
1616	LBSCR single bolster wagon	64
1619	LBSCR single bolster wagon	64
1641	LSWR road vehicle truck	68
1661	LBSCR/SR road vehicle truck	69
1676	LSWR machinery truck	70, 71
1681	SECR/SR machinery truck	71, 72
1682	SR well wagon	73
1701	LSWR gunpowder van	37
1746	SECR ballast hopper wagon	87
1748	SECR ballast plough brake van	82
1749	BR ballast plough brake van	82
1760	LBSCR/SR ballast brake van	84
1761	SECR/BR ballast brake van	83
1771	SR 5-plank ballast dropside wagon	91
1772	SR bogie ballast hopper wagon	89 – 91
1773	SR 4-plank ballast dropside wagon	93
1774	SR bogie ballast hopper wagon	90
1775	SR bogie ballast hopper wagon	90
3011	SR K-type container	80
3018	SR BK-type container	80
3026	SR BD-type container	77
3028	SR BK-type container	79
3091	SR Channel Ferry guard's van	106
3092	SR guard's van	108, 109
3093	SR/BR bogie guard's van	109
3098	SR bogie corridor luggage van	119
3099	SR bogie corridor luggage van	119
3100	SR bogie corridor luggage van	119
3101	SR/BR covered carriage truck (general utility van)	127, 128
3103	SR/BR luggage van	121
3105	SR luggage van	123
3141	SR/BR special cattle van	33
3152	SR fixed milk tank wagon	135
3154	SR 6-wheeled mobile tank carriage truck	134
3155	SR 6-wheeled fixed milk tank wagon	136
3156	SR 6-wheeled fixed milk tank wagon	136
3157	SR 6-wheeled fixed milk tank wagon	136
3159	SR 6-wheeled fixed milk tank wagon	135
3181	SR bogie covered carriage truck (scenery van)	129
3182	SR/BR bogie covered carriage truck (scenery van)	129
3183	SR/BR bogie covered motor car van	131
3191	SR bogie Post Office van (sorting)	145
3192	SR bogie Post Office van (sorting)	145
3196	SR bogie Post Office van (stowage)	149
1/034	BR 5-plank open goods wagon	8
1/035	BR 5-plank shock-absorbing open goods wagon	10
1/202	SR/BR covered goods wagon	23
1/351	SR/BR large cattle wagon	35
1/570	SR/BR steel-sided ballast dropside wagon	94
1/574	BR steel-sided ballast dropside wagon	94
1/580	BR ballast hopper wagon	87
1/583	BR ballast hopper wagon	87
1/584	BR ballast hopper wagon	87
3/049	BR B-type container	79
3/051	BR BD-type container	77
3/125	BR container	79
3/126	BR container	79
3/127	BR container	79